SAMENESS IS OUR STRENGTH

The Need for Nationalism and a Common Culture

SAMENESS IS OUR STRENGTH

The Need for Nationalism and a Common Culture

Adapted from Part Three of ***CHRIST OR COLLAPSE:***
The Case Against Godless Government

DAVID MILLARD HASKELL

The audiobook for this work, other shorter, excerpted editions, and the full version of *Christ or Collapse* are available at **CollegePress.com**

College Press Publishing
1307 W 20th Street
Joplin, MO 64804
www.collegepress.com

Adapted from Part Three of
Christ or Collapse: The Case Against Godless Government

Library of Congress Cataloging-in-Publication Data

Names: Haskell, David Millard, 1968– author.
Title: Sameness is our strength : the need for nationalism and a common culture / David Millard Haskell.
Other titles: Christ or Collapse. Part three. Adapted.
Description: First edition. | Joplin, Missouri : College Press Publishing, 2026. | Adapted from Part Three of Christ or Collapse: The Case Against Godless Government. | Includes bibliographical references.

Identifiers: ISBN 978-0-89900-469-3 (print) | ISBN 978-0-89900-475-4 (e-book) | ISBN 978-0-89900-481-5 (audiobook)

Subjects: LCSH: Nationalism—United States. | National identity—United States. | National identity—Canada. | Cultural pluralism—United States. | Cultural pluralism—Canada. | Immigration—Social aspects—United States. | Immigration—Social aspects—Canada.

Classification: LCC JC311 2026 (print) | LCC JC311 (e-book) | LCC JC311 (audiobook) | DDC 320.54

Contents

Introduction

This book, *Sameness Is Our Strength: The Need for Nationalism and a Common Culture,* is an excerpt from the larger work, *Christ or Collapse: The Case Against Godless Government.*

In total, four shorter volumes, each containing two to four chapters from the larger work, have been created. Because this book is an excerpt, readers will occasionally encounter references to ideas or remarks found in chapters not included here. Though this may at times give pause, such references can be safely overlooked, as no essential concepts required to understand this volume are missing, and the discussion remains complete and intelligible on its own.

This compact volume you're about to read brings together Chapters 7 and 8—which comprise Part Three of *Christ or Collapse.* Like all the shorter books in the series, it begins by defining the political philosophy of Traditional Conservatism and outlining its core principles, clarifying that its aim is for Christian norms and values to inform governance. Next it provides a clear explanation of healthy nationalism, then presents extensive research showing that mass immigration can significantly undermine a nation's safety, civility, and economic stability. It concludes with strategies for building a common culture that can restore unity in the United States and Canada.

If you find the ideas in this volume compelling, I encourage you to continue with the other excerpts in the series or the full text itself. All are available as books or audiobooks.

The first volume in this collection of shorter works, titled *Our Foundation for Flourishing: Christianity's Positive Influence on Government and Society*, presents Part One of *Christ or Collapse* and is comprised of Chapters 1, 2, and 3. After defining the core tenets of Traditional Conservatism, it demonstrates that the philosophy's mission to have Christian norms and values shape the nation's laws is nothing new. In fact, it has been the default position of both America and Canada since their respective beginnings. The book concludes by presenting a vast array of studies demonstrating the unique social benefits associated with the practice of Christian norms and values. By providing empirical evidence of the good produced by these norms and values, it supports Traditional Conservatism's call for those principles to again guide public life and policy.

The second excerpt in the series is titled *Our Unanchored Society: How Progressivism, Classical Liberalism, and Libertarianism Have Set Us Adrift*. It presents Part Two of *Christ or Collapse* and combines Chapters 4, 5, and 6. It traces the historical development of progressivism and other liberal ideologies, then, drawing on empirical evidence, it examines the damage that occurs when the "social justice" of progressivism replaces genuine justice. It concludes by showing how the "unrestrained freedom" championed by Classical Liberals and Libertarians is a pathway to enslavement.

The final volume in the series, features Chapters 9, 10, 11, and 12—which together comprise Part Four of *Christ or Collapse*. Following the principles and aims of Traditional Conservatism, it then explores the deeper theological foundations that undergird the philosophy and explains how traditional conservative laws from the past can serve as a blueprint for the present. The discussion also addresses why the Christian moral framework of Traditional Conservatism is incompatible with certain actions and policies currently sanctioned by the state. The volume concludes by outlining practical strategies for advancing Traditional Conservatism today.

At the end of every shorter volume—and also at the end of the full work, *Christ or Collapse*—I've included a two-page Postscript that invites those persuaded by the ideas of Traditional Conservatism to join with others who share their conviction. Perhaps I'll be hearing from you.

In the meantime, I hope you enjoy *Sameness Is Our Strength: The Need for Nationalism and a Common Culture.*

1

Principles of Traditional Conservatism

The Advantages and Disadvantages of Excerpts

As the cover of this book—and the Introduction you just read—makes clear, this volume is an excerpt from the larger work *Christ or Collapse: The Case Against Godless Government*. The full book develops its argument across more than 550 pages and draws on over 1,000 corroborating references, bringing together historical analysis, philosophical reasoning, and empirical evidence. An excerpt like this allows readers to engage deeply with one important portion of that broader argument—perhaps an area that particularly interests them. In that sense, it serves both as a lens and a gateway: it offers a focused look at one major theme while also inviting readers to explore the full work for a more comprehensive understanding.

At the same time, reading an excerpt from a larger work has its limitations. In the full book, many of the central ideas and assumptions are introduced and developed earlier. When a shorter volume is drawn from later chapters of a much larger work—as this one is—some of that earlier conceptual ground-work is necessarily absent. As a result, readers may encounter later arguments whose deeper foundations were laid out earlier in the first few pages.

To address this and fill in the most likely definitional gaps, this chapter—Principles of Traditional Conservatism—introduces several of the key ideas from the introductory pages of *Christ or Collapse*. These provide the philosophical tenets that inform the arguments developed throughout the book. By outlining them at the start, readers are given the essential framework needed to understand the analysis that follows.

One final point deserves special attention. Because nationalism is the main focus of this shorter volume, readers should pay close attention to one key section in this chapter. Below, in the list of tenets associated with Traditional Conservatism, the fifth item—Promotion of Nationalism—is especially important. It provides the core ideas that support the more detailed arguments developed throughout the rest of this book.

Readers who want to move quickly to this book's main arguments about nationalism, a common culture, and immigration reform in North America may be tempted to skim this chapter. Skim if necessary—but do not skip the section on Promotion of Nationalism. It lays the foundation for the arguments that follow.

Introducing Traditional Conservatism

This book champions Traditional Conservatism as a distinct political philosophy, separate from Christianity as a religious system. Though related, they are not identical. One need not believe the supernatural claims of Christianity to embrace Traditional Conservatism. However, one must believe the evidence that societies thrive—achieving peak individual freedom, social cohesion, and economic prosperity—when they adhere to a Christian ethos.

In straightforward terms, Traditional Conservatism holds that

Christian norms and values should shape a nation's practices and policies. It recognizes that laws cannot be ethically neutral—all laws mandate some kind of moral stand—and therefore it forthrightly requires that laws, explicitly and implicitly, reflect Christian morality (because it produces the best results).

At the same time, the philosophy holds that government leaders must acknowledge society's pluralism and respect the electorate's preferences regarding how Christian norms and values are translated into law. For example, the electorate signals whether laws and policies informed by Christian biblical standards should directly cite Scripture or theology. Also, respectful of today's ideologically diverse society, Traditional Conservatism holds that laws should incorporate natural law principles or be supported by appeals to logical reasoning and empirical evidence—rather than resting solely on "because Scripture says so."

What is not negotiable for a democratically elected traditional conservative government is the legalization or endorsement of what historical Christianity has consistently prohibited.

While advocating for laws rooted in Christian principles, this philosophy also maintains that the nation's statutes must respect the freedom of conscience of non-Christians and must not compel adherence to any particular religious belief. However, freedom of conscience and religion does not extend to groups or movements that promote violence or seek to overthrow Christianity or the traditional norms, values, and culture of the West. Freedom of conscience and religion protects only those who practice their faith—or no faith at all—without attacking the civilizational foundations of the nation. Apart from that caveat, under Traditional Conservatism, laws that steer society's actions toward the common good are acceptable; those that compel individual belief are not. In this, the philosophy safeguards the distinction between public and private spheres, ensuring the state's role is primarily confined to the former.

By insisting that the state's role be strictly limited to a few essential areas of public concern—and should not extend to controlling thought or imposing religious beliefs—Traditional Conservatism draws extensively from some of the key principles of Reformed Protestant theology. And while certain theological notions underpin much of Traditional Conservatism, its broader definition lets anyone—Christian or not—adopt it as a rational choice based on a preponderance of facts, not compelled faith. Through historical and empirical examples, traditional conservatives demonstrate to those who will listen that their political philosophy surpasses others in promoting societal well-being; it's on this evidentiary foundation that they present their argument for public consideration.

Furthermore, as it is explained in these pages, Traditional Conservatism as a political philosophy need not be linked to any specific political party. Throughout Western history, there have been various parties that did not carry the "conservative" label yet still upheld the principles of Traditional Conservatism. Many politicians touted as "liberal" years ago would qualify as traditional conservatives today, even if only in part. On the flip side, many established political parties that include "conservative" in their name today don't uphold the core tenets of the philosophy. Therefore, for the greatest clarity, remember that the true measure of Traditional Conservatism is the degree to which a party, politician, or individual aligns with the core principles of the philosophy outlined in this chapter.

Since Christianity and Traditional Conservatism are so closely interwoven, readers should expect frequent detours in these pages where

I emphasize unpacking the faith more than the philosophy itself. As the two are inseparable companions, it's worth noting that when I show how Christianity—through its orthodox values and practices—surpasses other religious and ideological systems in promoting societal well-being, this conclusion applies equally to Traditional Conservatism.

Put simply, Christianity is the soul animating the body of Traditional Conservatism, so exploring the societal benefits that the faith yields also reflects the benefits that Traditional Conservatism provides. To champion Christianity is to champion Traditional Conservatism—they rise together. As Christianity grows, so does Traditional Conservatism. I've pointed out that you don't need to be a believer to adopt this political philosophy; yet, when both heart and mind align, embracing it becomes more likely, and one's dedication to the cause grows far more passionate.

Why "Traditional Conservatism"?

I deliberately use the term "Traditional Conservatism" to distinguish it from contemporary political ideologies that label themselves "conservatism" yet diverge from, or even contradict, the foundational traits of the original political philosophy. For example, in some cases, Neo-Conservatism has been little more than warmongering to aid globalist imperialism. The Traditional Conservatism I endorse is grounded in British common law and Christianity, in particular, Reformed Protestantism. However, I believe that a devout Catholic who appreciates Thomistic thought would find this perspective largely in harmony with their own. Traditional Conservatism *conserves* those *traditions* of British law and Christian belief; other "conservatisms" do little or nothing to maintain the enduring moral order and divine intent that ground a stable society.

I explain Christianity's influence on this political philosophy in detail starting below and then throughout this book. Conversely, I will describe how British common law inspires Traditional Conservatism only briefly.[1] In short, common law provides a framework for turning the customs of a nation's people—worked out incrementally over time—into the official law of the land. From the Middle Ages, judges traveled throughout Britain, resolving disputes based on local conventions. Their rulings set precedents, ensuring consistency across similar cases. This incremental process transformed informal customs into a coherent legal system known as common law.

British common law, by valuing established customs, opposes the swift imposition of rigid decrees by a small elite driven by new theoretical ideas (something that's the norm today). That is to say, in its practice and process, judges do not seek to change popular custom to conform to their own world-view and sensibilities; instead, they work to protect popular custom by establishing legal precedents based on those time-honored traditions. This bottom-up approach—this judicial acquiescence to the people's prerogative—led British common law to gradually adapt in order to protect individual rights like property, liberty, and fair hearings.

It's important to note that many of our most valued legal protections grew out of the Christian-influenced customs of the British people. In other words, in England, customs based on a biblical understanding of individual and community life developed first. Historians tell us that the biblical worldview was widely accepted by the Norman Conquest in 1066,[2] and even earlier—about two centuries before—under Alfred the Great and his immediate successors.[3] Because the Bible emphasizes property rights, personal liberty, and fair hearings, British customs came to reflect these values. When judges later codified these customs into common law, they effectively enshrined biblical principles.

Though Traditional Conservatism originated in Britain, this philosophy has been embraced and refined across the Anglosphere in nations historically linked to the UK and predominantly English-speaking, such as the United States, Canada, Australia, and New Zealand. As these countries attest—at least historically—the success of Traditional Conservatism lies in its ability to adapt and evolve for the common good while preserving core truths, a balance made possible by blending British common law and Christianity.

Below, I'll list and explain nine of the core tenets of Traditional Conservatism. My list of Traditional Conservatism's traits is by no means exhaustive. Many before me have compiled their own definitions of conservatism, often including a broader range of points. Notably, the influential American political theorist Russell Kirk articulated ten principles of conservatism,[4] and these were, in large part, a distillation of the tenets that Englishman Edmund Burke put forward in the late 1700s.[5] That said, I'm confident that my version would not be found lacking by Kirk, Burke, or other foundational thinkers. Though my language and emphasis may differ, the underlying philosophy remains unmistakably aligned.

Core Tenets of Traditional Conservatism

1. Traditional Conservatism Relies on Christian Moral Absolutes

As I've suggested, the paramount feature of Traditional Conservatism is its unwavering dependence on the moral absolutes of Christianity for civic direction. Christian norms and values serve as the unchanging, non-negotiable touchstones by which all other elements of public life must ultimately orient themselves. Importantly, they are the ground from which all other elements of the political philosophy grow. Supported by historical and current evidence, the philosophy contends that a society lacking laws rooted in Christianity's moral absolutes inevitably falls into moral relativism and disorder or becomes tyrannical.

As I enumerate each of the other tenets of Traditional Conservatism, I'll touch on how they originate in scripture. I'll also mention that by explicitly linking Traditional Conservatism to Christian doctrines, my presentation of this political philosophy stands apart from most contemporary voices. In fact, my account may strike some readers as more overtly religious than even the works of Edmund Burke or Russell Kirk—Christians both, and the foremost architects of this philosophy. I attribute that difference to historical context.

Writing in the late 18th and mid-20th centuries, respectively, Burke and Kirk could assume their readers were already steeped in Christian belief and ethics—they took for granted the moral absolutes of the faith. Thus, when Burke affirmed that conservatism is rooted in "one law for all, namely that law which governs all law, the law of our Creator,"[6] and Kirk declared that "the conservative believes that there exists an enduring moral order. That order is made for man, and man is made for it: human nature is a constant, and moral truths are permanent,"[7] neither found it necessary to elaborate on who the Creator was or what His moral law entailed. Additionally, Kirk's reluctance to explicitly acknowledge conservatism's debt to Christian doctrine may reflect the cultural climate of his time. In the aftermath of World War II, even among conservatives, there was a growing tendency to downplay overt references to Christianity in public discourse—viewed as a way to promote broader social cohesion in an increasingly pluralistic society. As society careens toward the abyss, we now recognize the folly of that notion. Today's Traditional Conservatism begins by acknowledging its reliance on Christian doctrine.

2. Reluctance to Abandon Established Customs and Traditions

As a political philosophy, Traditional Conservatism posits that society's customs and traditions have developed for good reason: their longevity implies usefulness. Therefore, it advises skepticism when faced with the radical removal of norms and values that have stood the test of time. Following this same line of thought, the philosophy holds that traditions and customs provide a nation with stability, continuity, and a sense of identity and belonging. This isn't to say that the philosophy prohibits or avoids change. Change is welcome when it meets the following criteria: it follows prudent deliberation; it's a response to proven necessity, such as the elimination of explicit harm; it works to restore tradition; and, importantly, it doesn't erode established moral absolutes.

This political tenet—continuity of custom—finds its inspiration in Christian doctrine. To trace the line back further, Christian doctrine itself is grounded in God's Word as revealed in the established texts of the Old and New Testaments. Among God's people, therefore, the order has consistently been this: God's Word gives rise to doctrine, and doctrine gives rise to enduring custom.

For example, in Matthew 22:37–40, summarizing the core commandments, Jesus says: "'Love the Lord your God with all your heart and with all your soul and with all your mind.' This is the first and greatest commandment. And the second is like it: 'Love your neighbor as yourself.' All the Law and the Prophets hang on these two commandments." This divine command became, in very large measure, custom across the West.

Some have misinterpreted scripture to argue that Jesus' mission was to tear down established tradition. This is not so. Jesus himself addressed this issue, saying, "Do not think that I have come to abolish the Law or the Prophets; I have not come to abolish them but to fulfill them. For truly I tell you, until heaven and earth disappear, not the smallest letter, not the least stroke of a pen, will by any means disappear from the Law until everything is accomplished" (Matthew 5:17-18). When one examines the examples that supposedly suggest that Jesus was intent on tearing down tradition, it's clear that his efforts were not to override but to restore, correcting people's flawed understanding of ancient wisdom and custom so they might follow them better (for example, Matthew 5:21, 43).

Apart from the words of Jesus found in the Gospels, other books of the New Testament call for the veneration of inherited insight and practice. In 2 Timothy 3:16-17, the early church leader, the Apostle Paul, celebrates the tradition of the faith as a timeless guide for human life, writing, "All Scripture is God-breathed and is useful for teaching, rebuking, correcting and training in righteousness, so that the servant of God may be thoroughly equipped for every good work."

Elsewhere, in Romans 1:21-22, Paul warns that turning away from God's established law results in both moral and intellectual decline. Similarly, James 1:25 praises those who persevere in following divine norms and values, highlighting the benefits that arise from adherence: "But whoever looks intently into the perfect law that gives freedom, and continues in it—not forgetting what they have heard, but doing it—they will be blessed in what they do." By extension, scripture proposes that people find unity in their common adherence to core beliefs and time-honored standards (for example, Galatians 3:28).

Old Testament scriptures equally underscore the enduring authority of ancient instruction, portraying it as a sacred inheritance to be honored and upheld. For example, veneration of ancient wisdom is vividly expressed in Psalm 119, a lengthy hymn of devotion to God's law. Verse 97 declares, "Oh, how I love your law! I meditate on it all day long," while verse 105 states, "Your word is a lamp for my feet, a light on my path."

Similarly, Deuteronomy 4:5-6 reinforces this reverence when the prophet Moses instructs the Israelites: "See, I have taught you decrees and laws as the Lord my God commanded me, so that you may follow them in the land you are entering to take possession of it. Observe them carefully, for this will show your wisdom and understanding to the nations, who will hear about all these decrees and say, 'Surely this great nation is a wise and understanding people.'" In this context, following God's ancient statutes transcends mere legal duty, serving as the foundation for a nation's identity and a shining example to others.

Later, in Deuteronomy 6:6-7, Moses instructs the Israelites, "These commandments that I give you today are to be on your hearts. Impress them on your children. Talk about them when you sit at home and when you walk along the road, when you lie down and when you get up." This passage underscores the duty to safeguard the spiritual heritage—the commandments and promises given to their forefathers—by passing them intact to the next generation. Psalm 78:4-6 expands this vision, declaring, "We will not hide them from their descendants; we will tell the next generation the praiseworthy deeds of the LORD, his power, and the wonders he has done ... that the next generation might know them, the children yet unborn, and arise and tell them to their children."

3. Obligation to Ancestors and Descendants—Stewardship of Inheritance

As touched on previously, much of Traditional Conservatism is influenced by Englishman Edmund Burke (1729-1797), who emphasized the importance of "the contract of eternal society."[8] His notion indicates that society is a partnership between those who are living, those who are dead, and those who are yet to be born. The traditional conservative principle of cherishing ancient traditions, norms, and values—explained just above—is one aspect of Burke's concept. However, in addition to passing down intangible cultural treasures to provide an ethereal sense of belonging across generations, Burke also envisioned the protection of tangible assets as part of his contract. That is, beyond specific custom, concrete holdings such as land, resources, or institutions that tangibly scaffold the foundations of society must be protected and preserved.

This protection and preservation are not optional but an obligation to one's forebears arising from gratitude for the material benefits they have bequeathed. The current generation, knowing they are enjoying the fruit of trees they neither planted nor brought to full bloom, feels duty-bound to ensure those tangible treasures are not neglected or given to strangers with neither history nor love for them. Instead, they must devotedly tend and even multiply them for the countrymen who follow. From the perspective of the forebearers, they can feel contented knowing that what they sacrificed to achieve will not be lost; their sentiment is: "I'm pleased to leave you this treasure; all I ask is that you take care of it."

While Traditional Conservatism insists that the current generation of countrymen is obligated to protect and preserve the land, resources, and institutions created and enhanced by past generations, it recognizes that this mission is significantly compromised when a population is overwhelmed by newcomers with no connection to the builders of the civilization. Newcomers may feel an obligation to the ancestors of their own birthplace, but they have little emotional connection to the deceased citizens whose work and sacrifices created the new environment they now enjoy. With no historical connection, there is no contemporary obligation.

To address this problem—to ensure that the duty to past generations is fulfilled and the tangible resources created by previous countrymen are not squandered or lost—leaders within the Traditional Conservatism movement are beginning to contemplate an expansive notion of rightful inheritance. While the details are slowly emerging, a society should recognize, as a starting point, that past public contributions must have a bearing on present and future public benefits. A family or group that has, for generations, given their time, talents, and treasure to establishing an outpost of civilization—through clearing land, constructing roads and buildings, creating community organizations, and contributing to public projects through decades of taxation—should have their historical and current involvement honored.

Their voice in public matters—especially those related to preserving what they and their ancestors produced over generations—should be given more recognition and sway. Exactly how this should be done is a point of debate. This sentiment reasserts itself in the philosophy's core principle of nationalism, and thus it will be explored more fully there.

What is beyond dispute is that those with deep emotional connections to land, resources, or institutions are more likely to preserve and protect them. One of the most powerful examples of deep emotional connection to the land leading to preservation and protection is found among hunters and anglers—most of whom lean heavily conservative and tend to have a longstanding connection to their native land. In the U.S., hunters and anglers have contributed more financial and physical support to wildlife habitats and management than any other group: "Sixty percent of budget funding for state fish and wildlife agencies, which are tasked with responsible wildlife management, is generated by hunters and anglers... Altogether, hunters pay more than $1.6 billion a year for conservation programs."[9]

Similarly, in Canada, hunters and anglers are the largest financial contributors to wildlife habitat conservation.[10]

In its emphasis on protecting the land and institutions passed down generationally, Traditional Conservatism parallels the Christian view of wise stewardship over what one is gifted. Scripture consistently frames this duty to preserve our ancestors' legacy and improve it for future generations as both a moral imperative and a covenantal trust. The sentiment is rooted in gratitude for what has been received and hope for what is yet to come.

The story of Adam and Eve in the Garden of Eden, as recounted in Genesis 1:26-28 and 2:15, serves as an early biblical example of human stewardship over the land, emphasizing both authority and responsibility. In Genesis 1:26-28, God creates humanity in His image and grants them dominion over the earth's creatures and resources, instructing them to "subdue it" and "fill the earth," which implies a role of active management and care rather than mere exploitation. This stewardship is further clarified in Genesis 2:15, where God places Adam in the garden "to work it and keep it," a phrase that combines cultivation (enhancing the land's fruitfulness) with protection (preserving its integrity). The narrative positions Adam and Eve as caretakers of creation, tasked with maintaining and improving the garden under God's guidance—until their disobedience disrupts this harmonious role.

Later in the Old Testament, this theme of inheritance as both a divine right and an obligation appears. In Numbers 27:1-11, Zelophehad, an Israelite man, dies without sons, leaving his five daughters. As women, there was dispute over whether they could inherit their father's land. God, through Moses, affirms their claim, ensuring that the material good accrued by prior generations is preserved for the descendants, rather than lost to those who contributed nothing.

Elsewhere, the Old Testament describes improvement for the future as a duty. Proverbs 13:22 states, "A good man leaves an inheritance to his children's children," suggesting that righteousness involves not only maintaining what was received but multiplying it for posterity.

The New Testament deepens this principle. The parable of the talents (Matthew 25:14-30) is commonly understood among Christians as a teaching that urges individuals to actively contribute to and enhance the world beyond what they inherit. The servants in the story are entrusted with their master's goods, expected not just to preserve them faithfully but also to multiply them wisely. The one servant who merely buries the coins he was given—preserving without improving—is condemned, while those who invested and increased their initial sum are praised. Beyond a strictly religious context, the moral lesson is that people have a duty to multiply the resources entrusted to them, improving the world and leaving it better than they found it.

4. Acceptance of Social Hierarchies

Traditional Conservatism is at ease with a hierarchical social order where roles and responsibilities are clearly defined and distributed according to natural competencies and records of greater obligation or sacrifice.

Regarding competencies, it admits that some are more suited than others to certain roles, and when character, capacity, and career align, stability, peace, and prosperity follow. To say that some are more suited than others to certain roles is to rebuke the notion that "all men are created equal"—at least as today's progressives would understand it.

Weaving a narrative fit for a fantasy or science fiction novel, progressives today promote the idea that innate differences between people are virtually nonexistent (with the exception that Whites are innately more racist). For them, it's not a lack of skills, talent, or competence that prevents certain people from occupying particular positions; it's systemic bigotry. Because they believe people are fundamentally equal, like identical twins, they conclude that if someone falls behind, the cause must be nefarious and social, not natural or individual.

This near-literal belief that people are innately equal inspires progressives to take dramatic corrective action, specifically calling for the removal of criteria based on merit and competency and the imposition of criteria based on gender, sexual orientation, or skin color. This often involves government interventions—such as affirmative action, diversity quotas, or wealth redistribution—to ensure equality not just in opportunity but also in actual outcomes across gender, racial, and social lines.

Traditional conservatives hold that the principle "all men are created equal" is fundamentally a legal concept—referring to equality before the law and in natural rights—rather than a claim about biological sameness or sociological uniformity. Therefore, enforcing equality of outcome is to do violence to the very principle of equality, undermining liberty and property rights. They hold that differences in talent, effort, and circumstance naturally produce varied outcomes, and that government should safeguard fairness, not force uniformity. It's not the business of the state to make people equal in fact, but to ensure that the laws are equal.

When hierarchies emerge justly based on merit, traditional conservatives maintain that, at the societal level, subordinates in fields such as business, religion, the military, or other institutions should willingly and harmoniously follow those in higher positions—except in cases where a superior commands actions that clearly violate established moral principles. Likewise, within the family, traditional conservatives—particularly those rooted in the Christian faith—affirm the husband as the head of the household and uphold the expectation that children honor and respect their parents.

This call to defer to those in leadership above you does not equate to support for oppression, but rather to honor given for greater obligation, respect for different societal roles, and a desire for optimal functionality. Related to the latter, from a leadership theory perspective, organizations and teams—even families—function best when there's a clearly recognized point of ultimate responsibility, ensuring decisive action and coherent direction. In terms of checks and balances, those who receive the elevated status that comes from greater authority only maintain that status and authority insofar as they willingly accept and fulfill their greater responsibilities. Key among their responsibilities is securing—through their own sacrifice if necessary—the best circumstances for those under their authority.

In all circumstances, Traditional Conservatism consistently honors sacrifice made in service to others, granting greater status and influence—essentially a higher place in the social hierarchy—as a key form of recognition. This approach reflects the Christian ideal that true greatness comes through selfless service, as Jesus taught: "Not so with you. Instead, whoever wants to become great among you must be your servant" (Mark 10:43).

At the societal level, the philosophy's acceptance of a ranked, social pyramid of positions reflects the Christian notion of believers forming the "Body of Christ," a hierarchical yet caring communal structure where everyone has a role that aligns with their natural abilities, fostering maximum benefit and mutual respect (for example, 1 Corinthians 11:3 and 12:12-27).

At the level of families, the notions of male headship and honoring of parents also have a Christian pedigree. Christian scriptures, such as Ephesians 5:22-24 and Colossians 3:18-19, emphasize that wives are to submit to their husbands as the highest authority in the family, portraying this dynamic as a reflection of Christ's headship over the church. Ephesians instructs wives to submit "as to the Lord," with the husband as "head of the wife," while Colossians reinforces this submission "as is fitting in the Lord," framing it as a divine order. However, this authority isn't absolute or oppressive; it's paired with the husband's obligation to love his wife sacrificially, mirroring Christ's self-giving love for the church, thus balancing headship with mutual care and responsibility. Related to honoring parents, Christians find this commanded in Exodus 20:12 and Ephesians 6:1-3, where obedience and respect are linked to God's design for family and societal stability more generally (a topic I'll return to in the next subsection).

Among the foundational principles of Traditional Conservatism, few provoke greater indignation from non-conservatives—and even from conservatives outside the traditional sphere—than the concept of hierarchy as it applies to a man being head of the household. Indeed, this concept of "male headship" clashes so sharply with modern attitudes that non-conservatives struggle to imagine even a single plausible justification for its legitimacy. While it's beyond the scope of this book to examine in detail the reasons why traditional gender roles promote societal flourishing, the books of George Gilder, in particular *Sexual Suicide*[11] and *Men and Marriage*,[12] provide fact-based arguments in support of that claim. More recently, Louise Perry's work *The Case Against the Sexual Revolution: A New Guide to Sex in the 21st Century* presents its own unique arguments for rejecting contemporary norms and values surrounding sex and relationships.[13]

5. Promotion of Nationalism

Nationalism, a core tenet of Traditional Conservatism, prioritizes the needs and interests of one's countrymen above those beyond the homeland's borders, reflecting a commitment to communal loyalty and sovereignty. Though not a perfect match, some substitute the term *fraternity* for nationalism when discussing this tenet of the philosophy—perhaps because it makes for better alliteration when grouping it alongside other principles of the philosophy like faith, family, and freedom. Fraternity refers to a sense of brotherhood, solidarity, and mutual support among members of a group or community with shared values. To feel a sense of fraternity, group members need not be direct kin, but because of their character and worldview, they share a bond as "your people." Whether using fraternity or nationalism as the descriptive term, central to this notion are the questions: "Who qualifies as one's 'countryman'?" and "What makes someone 'your people'?"

For Traditional Conservatism, a countryman starts with those holding official citizenship, but the right disposition is as important as proper documentation. The correct disposition involves embracing and defending the home nation's heritage—its language, culture, and historical traditions. In addition to documentation and disposition, the philosophy considers one's historical dwelling when assessing a countryman. It unashamedly proclaims that a multi-generational record of residence—with familial evidence of constructing and contributing to the infrastructure, community, and culture of a place—elevates one's status as a true countryman. As discussed previously, greater sacrifice (in this case, generational outlay to one's nation) also equates to greater honor within Traditional Conservatism.

A family or kin group that has proven its loyalty and commitment to the nation's well-being through decades or even centuries of sustained contributions deserves a stronger voice in shaping its future. Traditional Conservatism argues that the principle of "obligation to ancestors and descendants" demands such recognition, while the principle of "acceptance of social hierarchies"—in which greater contributions merit greater honor—justifies it.

However, building on the earlier discussion in the *Obligations to Ancestors and Descendants* section, this perspective does not endorse creating preferential laws or allocating additional public benefits to individuals based on their history of deep-rooted contributions to the country. Honoring them means giving their opinions, not their votes, greater weight. How this is to be done is currently a point of discussion among traditional conservatives and has not yet been resolved. What's becoming clear, however, is that the toil and treasure of decades—or centuries—are dishonored when they are casually handed over to those who neither appreciate nor merit them. That is to say, many traditional conservatives today maintain that something must be done to significantly slow current citizenship processes across the West.

A growing consensus holds that the current paths to citizenship in both the U.S. and Canada demand too little of newcomers. Granting insider status with such undue haste and with so little contribution from applicants is a humiliation to those who have given so much for so long. A more rigorous model that honors those who built the foundations we stand on demands an extended process toward citizenship—a decade or two is not unreasonable—during which applicants, and their families if applicable, must demonstrate successful assimilation and true allegiance. This dedication to their new nation is to be demonstrated not only in language and cultural customs but also through steady contributions to the tax base, the strengthening of social cohesion, and the betterment of their communities.

By contrast, those who refuse to adopt the national language or customs, or who prove to be financial burdens, social disruptors, or shirkers of civic duty, would be returned to their country of origin at the first clear evidence of a failure to integrate or provide a consistent net benefit to the nation.

In addition, even those who achieve citizenship after arriving from abroad must be restricted from holding government, military, or bureaucratic positions, and dual citizenship should be prohibited. While their second-generation descendants may participate, the original immigrants themselves cannot. These measures are not intended to judge ability but to ensure that key responsibilities remain in the hands of individuals deeply rooted in the nation's culture, history, and civic traditions. By tying governing or civic authority to long-term investment in the country, traditional conservatives aim to preserve stability and continuity while still allowing fully committed newcomers to earn their place as true countrymen once they meet all integration requirements.

Such requirements are hardly novel or unduly harsh, as they echo the standards imposed upon earlier generations of European immigrants who built the United States and Canada from their founding eras into the mid-twentieth century. With no government subsidies, welfare programs, or institutional safety nets to fall back on, their welcome was tacitly conditional: they were expected to labor, adapt, and contribute in ways that tangibly strengthened the societies they entered. In other words, belonging was never an entitlement but a covenant, sealed by the immigrant's ability to improve the nation that received them.

The greater honor given to a countryman because of his predecessors' longstanding loyalty does not diminish the legitimacy or fundamental rights of those who become citizens through the rigorous new extended process. Provided they meet the measures outlined above, newcomers become true countrymen. While they are not required to abandon the language or benign customs of their ancestral homelands, these must be secondary to the language, customs, and culture of their new nation. This full acceptance of the home nation's identity—combined with the rejection of political loyalties to former countries—transforms them from mere residents within the nation's borders to countrymen who embody the nation's established character. In expecting new citizens born elsewhere to assimilate fully, traditional conservatives express their desire for continuity through unity. What traditional conservatives are not expressing, however, is racism.

Whereas racism seeks to exclude based on immutable traits like skin color, nationalism, as promoted by today's traditional conservatives, ignores race as a divide and seeks to include anyone of goodwill through cultural assimilation. For the traditional conservative today, nationalism's impulse is based in collective allegiance, not biological determinism. A supporter of Traditional Conservatism of European background can easily share authentic fraternity with other countrymen who support the philosophy and hail from different ethnic backgrounds. If they share devotion to traditional Christian faith, the bond is even deeper, as they move from alignment of the head to alignment of the heart.

Currently, an overwhelming number of newcomers have taken up residence in countries of the West, and Traditional Conservatism's definition of nationalism provides a lens for assessing the success of that immigration project. Is there evidence that the masses of newly invited refugees and "citizens" embrace the nation's linguistic, cultural, and historical traditions as their own? Have they rejected political and cultural allegiances to any prior heritage? Are they making steady contributions to the tax base, the strengthening of social cohesion, and the betterment of their communities?

Perhaps more importantly, has anyone in authority asserted that they must meet those requirements? A traditional conservative leader would!

Naturally, the most reliable way for a country to ensure that newly arrived citizens fully adopt its linguistic, cultural, and historical traditions—while relinquishing political and cultural ties to previous heritages—is to primarily accept Christian immigrants. Traditional conservatives view this approach as not only reasonable but, given the current societal contexts of America and Canada—where many newcomers explicitly voice hatred for all things Western—essential. This theme will be explored in greater depth in the forthcoming chapters on nationalism.

Unlike some forms of nationalism, the nationalism promoted by Traditional Conservatism rejects racism because the philosophy aligns with Christianity. The faith clearly opposes racism, as demonstrated by key scriptural teachings affirming the unity and equal value of all people in Christ. Colossians 3:11 declares that in the new self, "Here there is no Gentile or Jew, circumcised or uncircumcised, barbarian, Scythian, slave or free, but Christ is all, and is in all," showing that racial distinctions are irrelevant in the process of sanctification and unity in Christ. Similarly, Galatians 3:28 states, "There is neither Jew nor Gentile, neither slave nor free, nor is there male and female, for you are all one in Christ Jesus," emphasizing equality across ethnic lines. Revelation 5:9-10 illustrates that Christ's redemption extends to "every tribe and language and people and nation," uniting diverse groups in worship and purpose. Ephesians 2:15-16 highlights the cross's role in abolishing enmity between groups, creating "one new humanity" through reconciliation. Finally, Deuteronomy 1:17 and Matthew 5:44 call for impartial judgment and love for all, condemning racial malice or pride as sin.

Other aspects of the philosophy's understanding of nationalism are also drawn from the Bible and Christian tradition. The Old Testament first justifies nationalism by portraying nations as divine inventions;

for example, Deuteronomy 32:8 reads, "When the Most High gave the nations their inheritance, when he divided all mankind, he set up boundaries for the peoples..." From the start, nations were presented as part of God's design to order mankind and allow diverse people groups to co-exist while retaining their unique languages or customs (for example, Genesis 10:31–32; Genesis 11:1-9; Psalm 86:9; Acts 17:26).

Related to the duty to prioritize one's countrymen over citizens of other nations, that notion begins in the Ten Commandments when God states: "Honor your father and your mother" (Exodus 20:12; Ephesians 6:2). Although this edict is primarily tailored to familial bonds, it lays the foundation for a greater sense of loyalty and re-sponsibility toward one's people, encouraging individuals to prioritize the well-being and stability of their own community before extending their concerns outward. Honor for forebears is linked to the sustain-ability of a nation, with God stating, "so that you may live long in the land the Lord your God is giving you." Sociological and anthropolog-ical research confirms that close-knit relationships based on ancestral connections provide the most solid foundation for social cohesion, reducing conflict and encouraging mutual support.[14]

Moving outward, the obligation to fellow citizens is explicitly com-manded in Deuteronomy 15:7-8: "If anyone is poor among your fellow Israelites [your countrymen] in any of the towns of the land the Lord your God is giving you, do not be hardhearted or tightfisted toward them. Rather, be openhanded and freely lend them whatever they need."

While the New Testament demands benevolence toward strangers (even one's enemies), the overriding obligation to first care for one's own people is reinforced. In Mark 7:9-13, Jesus condemns those who would allocate resources to other matters at the expense of their family.

Paul reiterates this principle, emphasizing that assistance to extended family and the larger Christian community takes precedence: the faithful are told to provide first "for their own relatives" (1 Timothy 5:8) and to prioritize good works "to those who are of the household of faith" (Galatians 6:10). From a Christian perspective, working to benefit one's country's citizens—especially the poorest and most vulnerable—is the clearest application of the golden rule: love your neighbor as yourself.

The traditional conservative's ideas surrounding who qualifies as a countryman and the obligations newcomers must meet to be considered legitimate citizens also have a biblical foundation. Scripture teaches that newcomers to an established nation must adopt the country's existing laws and customs to fully belong as citizens. This principle stems from a respect for God-given order, preservation of shared identity, and the need to guard against cultural erosion caused by those who reject or oppose the nation's social norms and values. The story of Ruth illustrates this principle when the eponymous Moabite immigrant vows to fully adopt Israel's traditions and faith, declaring: "Your people shall be my people, and your God my God" (Ruth 1:6).

The legal code of Judaism reinforces this principle. Leviticus 18:26 mandates that immigrants conform to the nation's laws: "But you must keep my decrees and my laws... the native-born and the foreigners residing among you." Similarly, Leviticus 19:33-34 instructs Israel to love sojourners (foreigners) and treat them fairly but also expects them to live as the native population.

In the New Testament, 1 Peter 2:13-14 commands: "Submit yourselves for the Lord's sake to every human authority: whether to the emperor, as the supreme authority, or to governors," framing obedience to a host nation's authority as an obligation. Additionally, scriptures such as 2 Corinthians 6:14-15, "Do not be yoked together with unbelievers. For what do righteousness and wickedness have in common?" and Ephesians 5:11, "Have nothing to do with the fruitless deeds of darkness," caution against associating with those who reject God's established principles. This suggests an obligation on longstanding citizens to develop strategies that will ensure newcomers embrace their nation's customs and traditions, which will safeguard the nation's traditional norms and values against erosion.

Like male headship, Traditional Conservatism's push for nationalism—especially a version insisting on one unifying culture—is resisted in a society steeped in the ideals of equity and inclusion. As one of the philosophy's most divisive tenets, nationalism earns a robust defense in two chapters of its own.

6. Support for Family

Although family may appear later in the list of characteristics, it holds paramount importance in Traditional Conservatism as a central pillar of support and emphasis. While the philosophy regards a Christian ethos as the intangible foundation of a thriving society, it views stable families as the tangible bedrock of social order. Families are the most basic social institution and serve as the primary training ground for positive civic engagement. For instance, children taught to honor their parents within the home learn to respect legitimate authority figures outside of it. Through family chores, they acquire a sense of duty that later translates into diligence in their external work. Daily interactions with parents and siblings foster teamwork, collaboration, and conflict resolution—skills that prepare them to navigate society more effectively. Above all, stable and loving families are essential for passing down customs and values, ensuring the continuity of cultural and moral heritage.

As is clear from the explanation above, Traditional Conservatism's elevation of family intertwines with its commitment to cultural continuity, hierarchical social order, and loyalty to one's countrymen. Given the profound good that flows from thriving families and their broader social impact, Traditional Conservatism actively supports their formation and preservation through political means, such as tax structures that benefit married couples, policies that elevate traditional marriage over other models and parental authority over state control, and governmental systems designed to strengthen rather than replace family life.

Traditional Conservatism's support for family is also grounded in scripture. In earlier discussions, we have already seen several biblical references affirming that family must be a priority (for example, Exodus 20:12; 1 Timothy 5:8). To these we may add the foundational teaching that marriage and children are central to God's purposes for humanity: "That is why a man leaves his father and mother and is united to his wife, and they become one flesh" (Genesis 2:24), and together they are commanded to "Be fruitful and increase in number; fill the earth and subdue it" (Genesis 1:28).

The primacy of parents in raising children is reinforced throughout scripture. Proverbs 22:6 captures the biblical vision of parents as divinely appointed educators, charged with "training their children in the way they should go." Deuteronomy 6:4–7 expands this responsibility, presenting the family as the primary vehicle for transmitting cultural, moral, and religious norms. God instructs parents: "These commandments that I give you today are to be on your hearts. Impress them on your children. Talk about them when you sit at home and when you walk along the road, when you lie down and when you get up."

The Apostle Paul echoes these principles in the New Testament, admonishing fathers: "Fathers, do not exasperate your children; instead, bring them up in the training and instruction of the Lord" (Ephesians 6:1–4). Here, Paul confirms the authority of parents while also emphasizing a balanced approach that fosters both spiritual growth and emotional well-being.

7. Limited Government

As seen above, Traditional Conservatism is dedicated to maximizing the social standing of the family; conversely, it seeks to minimize the size and role of government. Its call for limited government rests on two convictions: greater power breeds greater corruption, and a more active state produces a less active citizenry. In the former conviction, it mirrors the Christian teaching on humanity's propensity for sin (Romans 3:23); in the latter, the Christian teaching on industriousness and self-reliance (e.g., 2 Thessalonians 3:10–12; Proverbs 6:6–11; Ephesians 4:28).

That said, traditional conservatives hold that certain functions must remain within the sphere of government: the defense of the nation, the protection of individual rights (including the enforcement of contracts and security of property), and the maintenance of the rule of law through courts and law enforcement. Beyond these, responsibilities such as health care, welfare assistance, education, marriage licensing, and other social services are best shifted to families and churches (or other community organizations)—groups that, when freed from heavy taxation and burdensome regulation, can provide these services with equal or greater effectiveness.

In this respect, traditional conservatives share some ground with libertarians or classical liberals. Yet they depart sharply from the libertarian impulse to treat all rules as oppression. Conservatives are willing to assign government a more activist role in curbing depravity and encouraging decency for the common good, measuring both against the time-tested norms and values of Christianity.

The Apostle Paul's letter to the Romans (13:1–7) outlines the proper role of the state, and Traditional Conservatism aligns closely with his vision of legitimate and illegitimate power. Paul instructs believers—as a general rule—to submit to governing authorities, recognizing them as instituted by God to maintain order, punish wrongdoing, and promote the good of society. He also commends individuals to fulfill civic duties such as paying taxes and respecting rulers. Yet even here, the state's role is confined to upholding justice, maintaining order, and protecting citizens—functions that resonate with the limited-government convictions of traditional conservatives. Paul does not extend government's reach to economic redistribution, social engineering, or even education (which in modern contexts has often become the chief vehicle for social engineering).

Moreover, Paul's call to submit to rulers is not absolute. His command assumes that authorities act as "God's servant for your good" (Romans 13:4), fulfilling a divine mandate to promote justice and order. When a government departs from this mandate—commanding actions that violate Christian moral law or forbidding those required by faith, such as worship—the duty to obey shifts to a duty to resist. This principle is expressed in Acts 5:29, where Peter declares, "We must obey God rather than human beings!" affirming divine authority over human authority in cases of conflict (see also Exodus 7:14–18; Esther

5:1–2; Daniel 3:16–18; Daniel 6:10).

Thus, both Paul's instruction and Traditional Conservatism's view of the state rest on the same foundation: government is to be respected and obeyed insofar as it upholds justice and order under God, but it is never to be treated as an absolute power.

8. Support for Personal Freedom

I've just stated that Traditional Conservatism will employ the power of the state to curb or incentivize behavior in order to achieve the common good, with the "common good" understood as aligning with the historical Western-Christian worldview. Therefore, it may seem paradoxical to claim that this political philosophy also supports "maximum personal liberty." After all, to say that it's willing to use the state to discourage or encourage some behavior is to say that it's willing to quash the freedoms of those who want to do the opposite.

Incidentally, this is the major complaint of libertarians and classical liberals against conservatives, and it leads them to point a finger and scream, "See! They want to take away your freedom! They're authoritarians just like the Progressives!" However, this supposed contradiction can be reconciled by understanding two key aspects of traditional conservative thought.

First, Traditional Conservatism does not equate liberty with unfettered freedom but sees unfettered freedom as leading to slavery. At the individual level, uncontrolled freedoms lead to addiction, financial instability, criminal acts, relationship damage, social isolation, health issues, and failure to reach one's goals. At the level of society, to the extent that unfettered freedom creates masses of degenerate individuals with anti-social behavior, it creates dependent, dysfunctional, crime-ridden hellholes (think of cities with a long history of radical progressive leadership). Multiply the dysfunction caused by unfettered freedom to the level of a nation, and you create the preconditions for tyrants to rise. A population, desperate for order to be restored, is willing to exchange its rights for an assurance of safety and civility.

Rather than unfettered freedom, Traditional Conservatism advocates for "ordered liberty," where individual freedoms are balanced against the promotion of individual excellence and the need for societal stability. The philosophy defines maximum liberty as the most freedom each citizen can enjoy without undermining the social order, concluding that maximum liberty for the maximum number of people is only sustainable within a framework of laws, customs, and values informed by Christianity. However, as a safeguard against overcontrol and tyranny, the philosophy insists that this regulatory framework cannot be arbitrary or untested but must have a long record of balancing freedom against the maintenance of civil society. It will come as no surprise that traditional conservatives appeal to history to show that the laws, customs, and values formed in the Anglosphere under the influence of Christianity meet these criteria.

Beyond asserting that regulations informed by Christianity are best suited to maintain the balance between liberty and social order, Traditional Conservatism makes a related, yet more dramatic, claim. It posits that a citizenry immersed in the norms and values of Christianity is prone to self-regulation, honesty, cooperation, and responsibility. This leads to a society where individuals act in ways that naturally support social harmony, reducing the need for state oversight in personal conduct. In short, when sharing a "common moral language" supplied by Christianity, personal freedoms can be maximized because people do good and forgo evil of their own accord, requiring no external intervention.

From the Old Testament account of the Hebrews being led out of bondage in Egypt to liberty in the Promised Land, the Bible provides examples of how a people can and must be free. As with its other tenets, Traditional Conservatism's advocacy for and understanding of maximum liberty are dependent on stories and concepts from scripture.

The philosophy's position that unfettered freedom, or freedom out of balance, harms the individual and society is frequently attested in the Old and New Testaments, and it finds succinct expression in the Apostle Paul's first letter to the church in Corinth. After asserting that he has found true freedom in Christ, he details how that freedom must be used to become the best version of oneself, writing, "I have the right to do anything—but I will not be mastered by anything.... I have the right to do anything—but not everything is constructive" (1 Corinthians 6:12; 10:23).

Similarly, in 1 Corinthians 8:9, Paul discusses how one's freedom might impact others, warning, "Be careful, however, that the exercise of your rights does not become a stumbling block to the weak." He goes on to emphasize that those who are naturally self-disciplined or morally stronger should, for the common good, create a public environment that helps avoid the downfall of the temperamentally vulnerable (1 Corinthians 8:10-13; see also Romans 14:13–21).

One of the most iconic biblical passages on freedom is found in Jesus' words. In John 8:31-32, he declares, "If you hold to my teaching, you are really my disciples. Then you will know the truth, and the truth will set you free." On a spiritual level, this freedom delivers individuals from the bondage of sin, fostering a life-changing connection with God. However, on the level of personal character, this teaching echoes the traditional conservative vision of "true" freedom coming from the knowledge of the good, which allows individuals to realize their fullest potential, becoming their "best selves."

While the New Testament clearly defines freedom as liberation from sin or spiritual freedom rather than personal autonomy or self-governance, there are key passages where freedom is plainly extolled as the ability to act, speak, or think without restriction from external forces. In addition to his comments in 1 Corinthians mentioned above, in Galatians 5, Paul declares that Christians are to live freely according to their conscience guided by faith. In Romans 14 he discusses believers' freedom to choose their own course in matters not explicitly forbidden by scripture. His idea reflects Old Testament verses such as Deuteronomy 4:2, "Do not add to what I command you and do not subtract from it," which warn against human additions to divine law. The idea—that "Man should not legislate where God has been silent" or "Human laws should not bind where God has left men free"—became a key focus of early Protestant doctrine and continues to heavily influence Traditional Conservatism's approach to state restrictions on liberty.

The philosophy's emphasis on individual liberty and autonomy also finds inspiration and greater clarity in some of the other early doctrines of Protestantism—specifically *sola scriptura* and the *priesthood of all believers*—which emerged during the Reformation in the 1500s.

Sola scriptura teaches that the Bible alone is the ultimate authority in faith and practice, encouraging everyone to read and understand it independently. This opposed the Catholic view, which discouraged personal access to Scripture, maintaining that ordinary people should rely on clergy for interpretation. The doctrine of the *priesthood of all believers* states that every Christian, not just professional clergy, has direct access to God and is equally capable of serving him in their own sphere of influence. Together, these Protestant ideas helped shape Western values of individual liberty by democratizing religious knowledge, promoting literacy, and reinforcing personal agency.

In particular, by challenging the Catholic Church's exclusive authority, Protestantism encouraged individuals to scrutinize all forms of unchecked power and to expand their personal autonomy. This shift laid the groundwork for Enlightenment ideas about liberty, influencing Western societies to maximize individual freedoms. As Protestant reform spread, the resulting religious diversity and tolerance helped develop principles of pluralism and civil liberties, eventually shaping the legal and political frameworks that protect freedom of thought, speech, and religion.

9. Free Markets

Like personal freedom, Traditional Conservatism adopts a balanced view of free markets. It generally favors less government intervention, believing that greater personal autonomy leads to economic success. Its default stance, similar to libertarianism, is to let businesses and individuals operate with minimal regulation. However, it recognizes the need for controls to prevent obvious harm or injustice. When such controls are in place, it argues that a laissez-faire economy—a free market—encourages innovation, efficiency, and prosperity. In this system, the qualities, prices, supply, and demand of goods naturally self-regulate through competition.

But the philosophy holds that eroding social cohesion, compromised moral values, or significant threats to the welfare of the community justify additional regulation. Because of their dedication to the common good, their obligations to ancestors, and their patriotic duty to their countrymen, traditional conservatives often support solutions that are less profitable. They may enforce protections that, while costly, improve health or save historic sites. They may place the needs and desires of workers over those of business owners in certain employment disputes. Direct evidence of this is found in traditional conservatives' resentment toward monopolies, job loss through off-shoring, wage suppression due to labor oversupply, and job insecurity from restructuring or automation. In their inclination to put frater-nity before fortune, they are at odds with libertarians and even other types of conservatives.

At this stage of our exploration, we are starting to see some overlap. Astute readers will recognize that the Christian doctrines we have discussed in relation to other aspects of Traditional Conservatism also inform its stance on free markets. For instance, the stewardship principle (Genesis 1:28), where individuals are seen as caretakers of God's gifts, resonates with the economic activities in free markets by suggesting a duty to use resources in a way that makes them "fruitful and multiply." Rather than repeating these connections, I'll leave it to readers to revisit and link these ideas. Nonetheless, there are a few more Christian principles, not yet discussed, that support the free market perspective within Traditional Conservatism.

While Christians have occasionally chosen to hold property in com-mon and are always called to voluntarily use some of what they own to benefit others, they have also championed the right to private prop-erty. They recognize the importance of owning land and goods, as well as the freedom to produce, buy, and sell for personal gain. This position is a necessary precondition for free markets. For free markets to exist, a country needs a system where goods and services are traded. For a single market—or a broader market economy made up of many markets—to function, citizens must have secure property rights. One of the clearest endorsements of property rights in Christianity comes from the Ten Commandments, where "You shall not steal" (Exodus 20:15) inherently recognizes the right to property ownership. This commandment would be meaningless if there were no concept of personal ownership.

In Matthew 20:1–16, Jesus tells the parable of workers in a vineyard, each receiving wages according to their agreement with the owner. This parable acknowledges that individuals have the right to negotiate terms for their labor and that the vineyard owner has the right to manage his property as he sees fit. Elsewhere in the New Testament, Ephesians 4:28 states, "Anyone who has been stealing must steal no longer, but must work, doing something useful with their own ha nds..." Here, stopping theft is linked to the idea of working to gain personal property, which people are then free to use and share as they choose.

Moving outward to free markets, the Bible provides a moral framework within which market activities should operate. The core Christian principle for all economic endeavors is to work diligently for profits and to be grateful for them; this gratitude should then manifest as social responsibility and voluntary service to the community. For Christians, several biblical passages highlight ethical resource management. Proverbs 14:23 links profit to hard work, stating, "All hard work brings a profit, but mere talk leads only to poverty," endorsing industriousness in market economies. Jesus' Parable of the Talents (Matthew 25:14–30), mentioned earlier, underscores the rightness of investment and productivity being rewarded and advocates for entrepreneurship. Paul's teaching in 2 Thessalonians 3:10, "The one who is unwilling to work shall not eat," supports personal responsibility and a productivity-based livelihood.

Of course, the Christian teachings I've referenced do not detail the intricacies and operations of a modern economic system; however, they do align with free market principles of stewardship, the work–reward connection, and personal accountability.

Reasserting and Adding to the Purpose of this Book

The aim of this book is to persuade readers that the cultural revitalization and very survival of Western nations—especially the United States and Canada—depend on a majority of citizens pursuing Traditional Conservatism.

Traditional Conservatism is the application of Christian norms and values to the governance of a nation.

In the preceding pages, I've highlighted both the core tenets of this political philosophy and the ways in which the Christian faith supports and inspires them. As mentioned, in the pages that follow, not all of those tenets will be examined individually for their specific contributions to societal well-being. Rather, their significance will be conveyed through the cumulative weight of varied examples.

For most devout Christians, the information I've relayed in this chapter, including my major claim, will be met with affirming nods but little action beyond that. They will agree that the Christian faith holds the prescription for what ails society, but most will say they're too busy or too worried about public backlash to act on it.

By contrast, non-Christians are likely to reject my prescription for our ailing nations outright. No matter how concerned they are about society's decline, they would rather take a pass than support a project where Jesus is the de facto leader. After all, they think, what has He ever done for them?

The question is provocative—and unavoidable. It demands an answer.

Endnotes for Chapter 1

1. For a more complete description of the relationship of conservatism and British common law, see Yoram Hazony, *Conservatism: A Re-discovery* (Washington, DC: Regnery Gateway, 2022).

2. John Blair, *The Church in Anglo-Saxon Society* (Oxford: Oxford University Press, 2005).

3. S. Keynes and M. Lapidge, eds., *Alfred the Great: Asser's Life of King Alfred and Other Contemporary Sources* (London: Penguin Classics, 1983).

4. Russell Kirk, "Ten Conservative Principles," lecture, The Heritage Foundation, Washington, DC, March 20, 1986, ; also see Russell Kirk, *The Politics of Prudence* (Wilmington, DE: ISI Books, 1993); and Russell Kirk, *The Conservative Mind: From Burke to Santayana* (Chicago: Henry Regnery Company, 1953).

5. Edmund Burke, *Reflections on the Revolution in France*, ed. Conor Cruise O'Brien (London: Penguin Classics, 1986).

6. Edmund Burke, *The Works of the Right Honourable Edmund Burke*, vol. 7 (London: Henry G. Bohn, 1857), 90.

7. Russell Kirk, "Ten Conservative Principles," 3.

8. Edmund Burke, *Reflections on the Revolution in France*, ed. J. C. D. Clark (Stanford: Stanford University Press, 2001; originally published 1790), 261.

9. Rocky Mountain Elk Foundation, "Hunting Is Conservation," December 27, 2019, .

10. Canadian Wildlife Federation, *The Role of Hunters and Anglers in Conservation* (2018), .

11. George Gilder, *Sexual Suicide* (New York: Quadrangle/New York Times Book Co., 1973).

12. George Gilder, *Men and Marriage* (Gretna, LA: Pelican Publishing Company, 1986).

13. Louise Perry, *The Case Against the Sexual Revolution: A New Guide to Sex in the 21st Century* (Cambridge: Polity Press, 2022).

14. For example: Donna L. Leonetti and Benjamin Chabot-Hanowell, "The Foundation of Kinship: Households," *Human Nature* 22, nos. 1–2 (2011): 16–40, ; Benjamin Enke, "Kinship, Cooperation, and the Evolution of Moral Systems," *Quarterly Journal of Economics* 134, no. 2 (2019): 953–1019; Nicolette V. Roman et al., "Strengthening Family Bonds: A Systematic Review of Factors and Interventions That Enhance Family Cohesion," *Social Sciences* 14, no. 6 (2025): 371, .

2

We've Always Been a Nation of Immigrants (and other lies)

"But You Didn't Build the House Either"

In recent years, the United States and Canada have undergone immigration surges without precedent in their modern histories, overwhelming housing markets, healthcare systems, and economic resources. These outcomes are not accidental but the result of deliberate policy choices by Democratic administrations in the United States and Liberal governments in Canada—choices imposed in defiance of public will. No electorate consented to immigration at this scale. On the contrary, polling repeatedly shows majorities demanding substantial reductions, if not outright freezes.[1] The gap between voter preferences and government action shows a serious failure of democratic accountability. It suggests a troubling pattern in which left-leaning governments increase inflows, seemingly to expand their future voter base.

Progressive politicians have observed unmistakable demographic and ideological trend lines: native-born citizens—particularly young men—are shifting sharply toward conservative positions on issues like immigration, crime, and economic fairness.[2] Facing the potential loss of these voters, they have accelerated mass immigration as a strategy to bring in new populations who, once naturalized, are far more likely to vote for left-leaning parties than the existing electorate.[3]

There is one argument progressive leaders and their followers rely on above all others to challenge long-time, heritage citizens of the U.S. or Canada who call for strict limits on foreigners seeking to settle in their countries. I call it the "But you didn't build the house either" argument.

The idea is simple: heritage citizens—those whose family has lived in America or Canada for multiple generations—are told that because they did not personally create the country's wealth, institutions, or society, they have no exclusive moral claim to decide who may enter. In other words, inclusion at the end of long line of people who built a nation does not automatically grant you the right to exclude others who wish to participate. Framed this way, the argument underpins a more open approach to immigration, implying that restricting new-comers is unjust if no one "built the house" alone.

This analogy only appears persuasive because it treats a nation as some kind of abstract corporation or communal dormitory that be-longs equally to all mankind. However, once you recognize what a nation actually is—an extended family writ large, a kinship network stretched across centuries—the entire logic collapses, and the moral picture becomes clear.

Imagine a house built by your great-grandparents with their own hands on land they legally purchased or homesteaded. They raised the frame, laid the bricks, installed the plumbing, planted the garden, and paid the taxes for decades. When they died, they did not leave the house to random strangers; they deliberately passed it on to their children.

Those children did not cut the timber or fire the bricks themselves, yet no one seriously argues that they therefore lack the right to live in the house or decide who may enter it. When those children later pass the house on to you—their grandchild—you inherit it both legally and morally, even though you personally played no role in its original construction.

The house is yours not because you built it, but because it was built *for you*: through a continuous chain of labor, sacrifice, and intentional transfer across generations.

A country works exactly the same way, only on a larger scale. The institutions, infrastructure, rule of law, social trust, and prosperity you were born into are not a cosmic accident or an unowned resource that materialized out of nowhere. For heritage citizens, they are the accumulated capital of ten, twenty, or more generations of your ancestors who cleared the land, fought the wars, wrote the laws, paid the taxes, built the schools and hospitals, and—most importantly—chose to pass the resulting civilization on to their descendants rather than let it dissipate or be taken by outsiders.

Your citizenship is the deed to that inheritance. You didn't "build the house" with your own hands, but it was quite literally built for you by people who shared your blood, your culture, and your interests, and who explicitly intended you to have it.

The progressive argument only works if you pretend that inheritance itself is illegitimate—if you act as though, the moment the builders die, their life's work must revert to "humanity at large" instead of to their own children and grandchildren. But inheritance is one of the oldest and most universal principles human societies have ever recognized, precisely because it is the mechanism that turns sacrifice in one generation into security in the next. Without the assurance that what you build will go to your own posterity, the incentive to build anything lasting collapses.

So when someone tells an American or Canadian (or Frenchman, or

Englishman, etc.) "You didn't build that—you were just born lucky," the truthful answer is: No, I was not "just lucky." I'm the intended beneficiary of a multi-generational project carried out by people who followed my traditions, shared my values, and had my interests at heart. They conquered, settled, and civilized this land not for the abstract "humanity" that happened to be alive in their century, but for their posterity—me. My place of birth was not random cosmic dice; it was the deliberate achievement of my forefathers, and therefore my rightful inheritance.

The same is true for every people on earth. The Japanese inherit Japan because their ancestors built Japan for their descendants. Ethiopians inherit Ethiopia because their ancestors built Ethiopia for their descendants. There is nothing arbitrary or unfair about this order; it is the only order that has ever produced prosperous, lasting civilizations.

To those who insist the country you are born into is nothing but blind chance, the reality is far more profound: your place of birth is your achievement and your inheritance, paid for in the blood and toil of those who came before you—and now entrusted to you so that you may, in turn, pass it on undiminished to your own children. That is the moral claim no open-borders slogan can erase.

What makes progressives who diminish the standing of heritage citizens especially treacherous is their combination of hypocrisy and cultural vandalism. On the one hand, they argue that Americans and Canadians of European descent—whose families have lived, worked, and built institutions in these countries for generations—have no greater claim to the land than a foreigner who arrives today by boat or airplane.

On the other hand, these same progressives insist that Native Americans deserve unique distinctions, protections, and privileges unavailable to other citizens. Because they were here first, the argument goes, Indigenous groups may opt out of certain taxes and regulatory systems that bind everyone else. Governments are legally required to consult them—and in some cases obtain their consent—before developing public lands or approving major infrastructure projects. They also receive preferential access to government funding, along with dedicated political and legal arrangements not available to the general population. In Canada and the United States, specific benefits include exclusive resource rights, reserve lands held outside standard property law, separate court systems, access to additional healthcare services, Native-specific educational programs, benefits derived from tribal gaming enterprises and related revenue, and expanded hunting and fishing rights.

In the case of North American Indians, none of these distinctions are defended on the basis of universal equality. They are justified explicitly on ancestry, historical precedence, and inherited claims to land and authority—the very categories progressives deny when applied to heritage citizens of Western nations. Despite what they say, it's clear that progressives are not arguing for equality but for selective inheritance—applied when convenient and at the expense of the majority population and their heritage.

The irony is that traditional conservatives *could make* the case for greater rights for heritage citizens of the U.S. and Canada on the very principles progressives themselves routinely endorse, yet conservative nationalism today currently stops short of making that claim.

Fraternity, Patriotism, and Ordered Loves

The essence of nationalism, as it's defined and supported by Traditional Conservatism, is the prioritization of a nation's citizens over the interests of any individual or group from outside the country. It expresses a belief about how the world should be ordered. Most precisely, it holds that governing officials should craft the plans and policies of their nation to bring ultimate benefit to their own people—their countrymen. Chapter 1 provided a detailed explanation of who, according to Traditional Conservatism, qualifies as a countryman, so I won't address that again here.

What requires brief clarification is the difference between nationalism and patriotism. In chapter 1, I suggested that the term *fraternity* comes close—though imperfectly—to capturing the essence of nationalism. It conveys brotherhood, solidarity, and mutual support among those bound by shared values, yet it falls short of acknowledging a crucial element: the state's duty to deliberately advance the interests of its countrymen, even to the exclusion of others.

Patriotism shares a common spirit with nationalism but, like fraternity, is primarily inward-facing. It is the love, pride, and sense of indebtedness one feels toward one's nation and its people—a devotion rooted in memory, heritage, and shared sacrifice. Patriotism cultivates loyalty, gratitude, and a readiness to defend and preserve the community that has given us identity and belonging.

Nationalism, by contrast, gives that same affection political form. It is the outward-facing framework by which a people, usually through the state, deliberately advance the interests of their own countrymen—safeguarding sovereignty, securing borders, and promoting national flourishing in a world of other nations. In short, patriotism informs the heart; nationalism guides the body politic and the hand of policy.

As we have seen before, there are principles of Traditional Conservatism that exist in a healthy tension with each other. For example, Chapter 6 showed that the philosophy's emphasis on individual liberty is moderated by its sense of responsibility to the common good. In a similar way, Traditional Conservatism's understanding of nationalism tempers its commitment to free markets and shapes its approach to partiality in public dealings.

In economic matters, it holds that businesses operating within the nation should be subject to rules ensuring that they prioritize citizens over non-citizens. This might include discouraging or restricting companies from outsourcing production abroad or from hiring foreign workers. The goal is to ensure that economic activity strengthens the nation's workforce and serves its people first.

Likewise, in opportunities beyond employment—whether university admission, access to financial aid, housing, property ownership, or any other competitive arena—Traditional Conservatism holds that citizens should receive maximum priority. This perplexes some people. They wonder how traditional conservatives can insist that merit, not characteristics such as race, ethnicity, or sex, should determine success, yet also maintain that when the choice is between citizens and non-citizens, one must privilege one's own—even if the outsider has stronger credentials.

This is not hypocrisy but coherence when properly understood. Traditional Conservatism reconciles impartiality and partiality by assigning them to different moral domains. Impartiality governs relations among citizens; partiality governs relations between citizens and outsiders. In this way, the philosophy upholds both fairness and loyalty, seeing each as indispensable to the flourishing of a stable, cohesive society. In the eyes of traditional conservatives, the nation is a moral organism—an extended family maintaining established customs across generations—within which citizens are entitled to equal treatment under common rules. Yet just as no family is required to feed strangers before its own children, no nation is obliged to treat foreigners as though they were citizens.

As was demonstrated at length in Chapter 1, the notion of putting countrymen first finds its commendation and justification throughout the scriptures of the Old and New Testament. So ancient and well-established is this notion within Christian political thought that, as a theological principle, it has been enshrined under its Latin name: *ordo amoris*. Though the idea was present from the earliest days of Christianity, the first systematic account of ordo amoris—'ordered loves'—was given by St. Augustine in the 4th and 5th centuries, especially in his works *City of God* and *On Christian Doctrine*. Drawing on the same scripture that was referenced in Chapter 1, Augustine taught that a stable society depends on the right ordering of our affections. We must love things according to their true worth, with God as the supreme object of love. When God is rightly loved above all, one is then able to love in proper measure and in proper order. One's family comes first, followed by neighbors, then fellow citizens, and finally strangers. In *City of God*, Augustine offers an example of this graded duty of love as it flows from love of God:

> And this is the order of this concord, that a man, in the
> first place, injure no one, and, in the second, do good to
> everyone according to his reach. Primarily, therefore, his

own household are his care, for the law of nature and of society gives him more ready access to them and greater opportunity of serving them. And hence the apostle says, 'Now, if any provide not for his own, and specially for those of his own house, he has denied the faith, and is worse than an infidel.' 1 Timothy 5:8 ...[4]

Ordo amoris was later elaborated by St. Thomas Aquinas in the 13th century, who framed it as a "hierarchy of obligations" or "order of charity." Visualized as concentric circles radiating outward based on relational and physical proximity, he added more nuanced categories to Augustine's template: love God first, then oneself, family, extended family, close neighbors, community, fellow citizens, and finally the wider world.[5]

From the earliest Christians through Augustine and Aquinas to contemporary believers, the tradition has recognized a legitimate flexibility in cases of urgent need. For example, the obligation to assist distant strangers in grave peril—even at some cost to the comfort of one's own household—has never been in question. Nevertheless, in the ordinary course of life, the principle requires that affections remain properly ordered. To invert these priorities on a regular basis—treating the needs of those far away as equal to or greater than the needs of those nearby—undermines social cohesion and erodes the foundations necessary for the long-term practice of charity.

Why does tending first to one's own allow charity to endure? Because sustained charity requires resources to give, especially material resources such as income and savings. These resources are most reliably accumulated when parents are able to meet the needs of their children without being encumbered by prohibitive obligations to distant strangers. Children raised under such conditions are more likely to escape poverty and attain self-sufficiency. Having achieved stability, they in turn acquire the emotional, moral, and practical resources necessary to continue the practice of rightly ordered charity in their own lives. One cannot draw blood from a stone, just as one cannot draw charitable giving from those who lack the means to give. Former British Prime Minister and devout Christian Margaret Thatcher observed, "No one would remember the Good Samaritan if he had only had good intentions; he had money as well."[6] That money enabled him to provide charity for the man he found beaten on the highway.

A striking indication of the moral confusion pervading society is that politicians who argue that the needs of their own citizens should come first are often condemned. Shortly after taking office as Vice President of the United States, JD Vance appeared on national news to discuss limiting immigration as a way of prioritizing Americans. In support of his stance, he drew on the Christian theological concept of ordo amoris and criticized the political Left for inverting this order by prioritizing outsiders while neglecting or even disdaining their own countrymen.[7]

The comments quickly went viral on social media and sparked widespread denunciation from progressive commentators, especially theologically liberal Christians. To support their argument, these so-called "Christian" pundits distorted scripture—pulling quotes out of context—and acted as if Augustine, Aquinas, and the entire Christian political tradition had never existed.[8]

Disordered Loves and Societal Collapse

Ordo amoris as exercised within Christian nations throughout history has assisted in flourishing because it creates a unique moral balance. Human beings are naturally inclined to favor those bound to them by blood, community, and shared destiny. This is a primal instinct crucial to the sustaining of civilizations. Christianity did not seek to abolish this instinct but to moderate it, offering a noble corrective to the dangers of excessive self-interest and unchecked tribalism. It affirms that loyalty to family, community, and country are first obligations, yet insists that these must not come at the expense of compassion for the outsider. Assistance to those struck by misfortune through no fault of their own, including strangers in such circumstances, is presented not as optional but as necessary.

This Christianity-inspired compassion for the stranger extends beyond charity in day-to-day dealings. Teachings such as "Do to others as you would have them do to you" (Luke 6:31), together with the biblical commands to judge impartially (Deuteronomy 1:17; Leviticus 19:15) and to employ honest scales and honest weights (Leviticus 19:35–36; Proverbs 20:23), gave rise to something distinctive in the West. In addition to establishing the first and only high-trust societies in the history of the world—where contracts sealed with a handshake were honored and lost wallets were returned with cash untouched—an equally amazing merit-based system formed. Specifically, a civilizational framework arose where opportunities are extended fairly beyond one's own tribe to any *citizen* on the basis of merit and competency. Although not always applied perfectly to all citizens in all situations, the principle in the West has been: what you know matters more than who you know in opening doors.[9]

For example, American research from the late 2000s—before the onslaught of DEI measures—found that members of the majority White population, when tasked with hiring, were most likely to use neutral criteria—not ethnic markers—to make employment decision s.[10] The idea that "I will not advance my tribe if you agree not to advance yours" is more formally known as the *reciprocity norm*,[11] and social scientists note that its application is found almost exclusively in the West—especially in English-speaking countries shaped by a Protestant heritage.

On one front, this Christianity-inspired social equality is being eroded by progressivism's DEI regime—what you *are*, not what you *know*, is now a key variable in advancement. That is to say, the reciprocity norm—which ensured the best person would get the job—is being abandoned through the policy initiatives of the Left. However, on another front, that social order is being corrupted by a similar and equally damaging project of progressivism. We have acknowledged that, in the West, the doctrines of Christianity inspired a healthy softening of in-group loyalty. Preference for one's own tribe was mediated by a larger moral vision that allowed for the inclusion of any citizen, regardless of ethnic markers. However, with the advance of progressivism, that Christian-inspired "healthy softening" has metastasized into a formless moral mush. We've moved beyond a supple ripening to a collapse of structure itself—like a piece of fruit softened past usefulness into rot, incapable of holding its shape or sustaining life.

In short, we are witnessing an entirely new moral perversion that encourages longstanding citizens of the United States and Canada to put their own people second in a wide range of political, cultural, and economic decisions. Public intellectual and behavioral scientist Gad Saad describes this growing inclination to grant greater opportunity and more rights to those with no historical standing in one's country—and often with apathy or hostility toward its values and culture—as *suicidal empathy*.[12]

The ancient habit of tribal favoritism has given way to its radical inversion—an ideology that elevates the stranger above the neighbor, and the foreigner above the countryman. Enabling this inversion are decades of propaganda claiming that Western nations are morally inferior, while every non-Western nation is portrayed as morally pure and beyond criticism. Ironically, the West's markers of success are reinterpreted as moral stains: prosperity is cast as exploitation; wealth, achievement, and cultural influence become evidence of wrongdoing and oppression.

Different Attitudes Toward Love of Country and Countrymen

Through schools and media echo chambers, empathy for the outsider has been amplified into a sprawling, disordered virtue; concern for distant others is exalted, while obligations to kin, community, and nation are downplayed or dismissed. Even foreigners with ideologies and practices hostile to the West are extended uncritical approval and are often viewed more favorably than native, law-abiding citizens.[13] A groundbreaking 2019 study on ideological differences in the sphere of moral concern revealed a stark divide: conservatives and liberals direct their compassion toward very different groups within society.[14] Conservatives focus their deepest care on family, friends, in-groups, and nation, strengthening social cohesion and practical charity. Those on the political and social Left, by contrast, scatter their moral attention wide, extending concern to foreigners, animals, plants, and even abstract nature, often placing distant causes above their own country, friends, and family.[15]

The diminished love of country among self-identified progressives is evident in surveys on military service. When asked if they would defend their nation in the event of armed conflict, only about one-third of Americans and Canadians who describe themselves as "very liberal" or "progressive" say they would be willing to fight.[16] In contrast, more than two-thirds of conservatives answer yes, with those identifying as "very conservative" exceeding 70%.[17]

At the same time that significant numbers of North Americans are showing less loyalty to their native land and fellow countrymen, tribal loyalties elsewhere in the world remain deeply entrenched. From India to the Middle East to Africa, clan, caste, and ethnic ties continue to override broader social responsibility. Family and community connections are the currency that buys opportunities. Most native citizens of the West have no idea of the extent to which preferences for "one's own kind" are the dominant mindset in most of the rest of the world. For example, survey data collected by *U.S. News & World Report* and the Wharton School of Business at the University of Pennsylvania found that nearly half of Indian residents (44%) prefer associating with people of their own culture and ethnicity and feel uneasy around those from different backgrounds.[18] This result placed India at the top of the researchers' list of "most racist countries" in the world.[19] Although this attitude was measured within India itself, there is growing evidence that the same in-group preference persists among Indian immigrants living in the United States and Canada. It is not surprising that, because of mass immigration, these strong in-group loyalties are finding their way into Western societies, where they often go unchecked under the guise of progressive ideals. In America and Canada, for example, industries that employ managers from ethnic minority backgrounds—especially those from India—often experience rapid shifts in hiring, with favoritism flowing primarily to co-ethnics. The result, in certain workplaces, is the effective exclusion of individuals from the historic majority population.[20]

While co-ethnic hiring often goes unnoticed, an October 2024 federal jury verdict in the U.S. brought it into sharp focus. The jury found that New Jersey-based tech giant Cognizant Technology Solutions—led by Indian-origin executives—had brazenly prioritized Indian workers on H-1B visas over non-Indian employees, including American citizens, from 2013 to 2022. The court found that those non-Indian employees who did secure a position were later callously sidelined and terminated at far higher rates.[21]

Foreign Visas—Our Culture's Passport to Decline

Visas provide a particularly powerful case study on the in-group preference shown by many Indians. Recent investigations by U.S. Citizenship and Immigration Services show that H-1B visas are overwhelmingly awarded to Indian nationals, who received 71% of all approvals—far outpacing China's 11.7% share.[22] Much of this dominance arises from systemic cheating by major Indian outsourcing firms—perhaps reflecting cultural norms shaped outside the high-trust environment of the West. Companies like Infosys, Tata Consultancy Services, and HCL Technologies exploit the lottery system and regulatory loopholes to secure outsized numbers of visas, undermining fair competition and displacing American workers. Among their tactics is "multiple registration" fraud, submitting duplicate entries for the same worker to manipulate the lottery. While these firms have faced multimillion-dollar fines, the financial gains from their schemes often outweigh the penalties, allowing the abuses to continue largely unchecked.[23]

H-1B visas are not the only issue; another visa program worsens the imbalance. The F-1 visa, which applies to international students studying in the United States, gives foreign graduates a built-in financial advantage over American workers. Even without any ethnic favoritism, the system itself encourages employers to hire foreign workers. F-1 visa holders may work in the U.S. for up to 12 months after graduation—or up to 24 months in STEM fields—without them or their employers paying the payroll taxes that fund Social Security and Medicare.[24]

To put this plainly: employers save 7.65% of an employee's wages—their share of the payroll tax—every time they hire an F-1 graduate instead of a U.S. citizen.[25] Over several years, that "tax discount" turns into a powerful incentive to fill entry-level positions with foreign workers, all subsidized by a policy that makes native-born employees the more expensive choice. In effect, federal policy doesn't just tolerate wage displacement—it quietly underwrites it. Corporations are the big winners, able to boast about "global competitiveness" while paying a fraction of what labor really costs. Ordinary citizens are the big losers, left to "enjoy" the perks of diversity—fewer job openings, flatter wages, and a job market that seems to work for everyone except them. Again, no one voted for this. It was not debated or approved by the public. But corporations don't need votes when they can get what they want through backroom deals with politicians and campaign donations.

Just as certain visas in the United States are often used to promote minority in-group hiring, Canada's federal government operates two similar programs—the Temporary Foreign Worker Program (TFWP) and the International Mobility Program (IMP)—that allow businesses to hire immigrants over citizens. The TFWP permits employers to bring in foreign workers if they claim no qualified Canadians are available (a claim they always make but seldom support with evidence).

The IMP is even more permissive, letting companies hire from abroad without proving any labor shortage at all.[26] In practice, franchise owners and managers from certain ethnic backgrounds frequently recruit directly from their countries of origin, inviting co-ethnics to fill positions in Canada.[27] As seen in the U.S., this dynamic reduces opportunities for Canadians and pushes wages downward. To make matters worse, taxpayers are forced to finance much of it: public funds are used to support wage subsidies and training for these programs.[28] In effect, Canadians are paying for the very system that enables employers to replace them in their own labor market.

Government, courts, media, and academia in Canada work in concert to suppress discussion of issues like minority in-group hiring. As a result, cases of discrimination against the majority population rarely receive legal standing, academic attention, or press coverage. Yet some examples are too blatant to ignore. In-group hiring—especially among migrants from India—is common in sectors such as security,[29] towing,[30] and trucking,[31] but the most well-documented abuses occur within one of Canada's most recognizable brands—Tim Hortons coffee shops.

Despite South Asians comprising a small fraction of Canada's overall population, it has become routine to expect that in nearly all Tim Hortons, about 80 to 90% of employees will be of Indian origin. The factual basis for this observation is reinforced by stories from displaced employees—mostly White Canadians—who report being fired to make room for workers of Indian ancestry, most of whom are in the country on visas. For example, in the fall of 2025, several Tim Hortons franchises in Ontario drew national outrage after new owners abruptly dismissed long-time local Canadian employees and replaced them with temporary foreign workers from India. In Grand Bend, a small tourist town with limited year-round employment, the entire staff was fired just before the holiday season.[32] Similar terminations—Canadians turfed for foreign workers from India—occurred at four Tim Hortons locations in the town of Grimsby, Ontario. Only after a wave of public shaming on social media drew the attention of corporate headquarters was the decision reversed (at least for the time being).[33] In another bizarre case, a 17-year-old White, female Tim Horton's employee was pressured by her Indian manager to marry the manager's relative so that he might more easily gain permanent residency in Canada.[34] Many former employees have shared their stories online,[35] or, occasionally, through right-leaning media outlets willing to cover what mainstream sources avoid.[36]

These situations of minority in-group hiring provide a modern demonstration of how untempered tribal instincts can undermine the principles of fairness and civic unity that for centuries formed the bedrock of Western stability. When Traditional Conservatism insists that the state must prioritize its own citizens over foreigners, it does so in the knowledge that the opposite destroys social cohesion. Only when the state ensures that past contributions determine present and future benefits is the moral contract that binds a nation together preserved. When citizens see their efforts and sacrifices rewarded before the claims of outsiders, trust in institutions deepens, loyalty is reinforced, and a shared sense of destiny is maintained. But when the state abandons this principle—favoring non-citizens over citizens—gratitude and duty among the majority are replaced with resentment and alienation.

It stands to reason that if long-term taxpayers see their contributions diluted by policies that disproportionately reward non-contributors, they may reduce civic engagement, pay less attention to communal obligations, or even withdraw support from public institutions. Similarly, when communities observe an unequal distribution of benefits that ignores historical commitment, resentment can grow between groups, fracturing trust and mutual obligation. This erosion of trust impairs collective action: citizens are less likely to cooperate on shared projects, support public goods, or invest in future generations, knowing that the social compact no longer reflects merit, effort, or historical contribution.

Over time, such patterns can produce a cycle in which declining responsibility leads to weaker institutions, greater inequality, and diminished unity, undermining the very stability and prosperity that the state depends on for economic and cultural success. We will examine the proof of this later in the chapter.

The Myth of the Propositional Nation

In the section above, I briefly reflected on the method by which a large segment of the population can be persuaded to place the needs of their own countrymen second. A more extended reflection appeared in Chapters 4 and 5, where I explained how Marxist-influenced projects of social justice, diversity, equity, and inclusion—promoting resentment toward all things Western, White, Christian, or heterosexual—have cultivated growing indifference, and even hostility, toward one's own nation and fellow citizens. Given the extent of my previous exploration, one might think there would be nothing left to expose. Not so. There is yet another, equally insidious, form of propaganda that drives this erosion of national identity and, with it, civic duty. Our country's elites have redefined the United States and Canada as so-called "propositional nations."

At the heart of this deceit is the principle that simply espousing allegiance to vague Western values—not participating in shared traditions or a long, continuous history in a single place of origin—is sufficient to make one a true countryman. Critics like author and cultural commentator Douglas Murray suggest that support for the propositional nation rests on the illusion of "magic soil": the notion that mere presence on the land or nominal adherence to ideals magically transforms someone into an American, Canadian, or Englishman.[37] A contrast aids in understanding this concept. Other nations define themselves based on tangible realities. For example, Japan grounds national identity in centuries of shared language, culture, and ancestry; India weaves national identity from a complex tapestry of religion, caste, and historical communities; Saudi Arabia ties it to tribal lineage and adherence to Islamic norms. In these societies, being part of the nation is inseparable from being part of a people historically inhabiting the land. But this tie to tangible realities is abandoned under the banner of a propositional nation. In this model, anyone who tepidly supports such abstract concepts as liberty, equality, and democracy can, in principle, belong. National identity becomes a shallow, shared set of ideas, not a deep, shared set of experiences within an inherited community.

In the context of the United States, advocates of propositional nationhood argue that the country's identity derives from the principles articulated in foundational documents such as the Declaration of Independence, particularly the assertion that "all men are created equal" and are endowed with inalienable rights to life, liberty, and the pursuit of happiness.[38] They note that Abraham Lincoln famously reinforced this in the Gettysburg Address, describing America as a nation "conceived in liberty, and dedicated to the proposition that all men are created equal."[39] In this narrative, America's founding is portrayed as a deliberate act of propositional creation, distinguishing it from older nations historically bound by ethnic, religious, or cultural ties. The narrative falsely claims that the nation is not rooted in a particular people or culture but is an idea that, in principle, could be transposed to any place regardless of the population.

This conception, inaccurate as it is, strongly emphasizes the progressive values of inclusivity and universalism, as well as the libertarian focus on individual autonomy. In line with the latter, proponents argue that individuals—not groups, communities, or traditions—are the fundamental units of society, and that national unity emerges from voluntary agreement between independent beings sharing similar principles.

Similar arguments are made in Canada. Proponents point to the British North America Act of 1867 (now the Constitution Act, 1867), emphasizing that it establishes governance structures—parliamentary democracy, federalism, and the rule of law—rather than a specific ethnic identity, thereby implying that anyone who accepts these structures can be Canadian. They further note that the Canadian Charter of Rights and Freedoms, adopted in 1982, reinforced multiculturalism as a core national value, framing Canada as a nation in which adherence to democratic principles, rather than custom or ethnicity, defines belonging. Moreover, the official policy of multiculturalism rejects the notion of a singular "Canadian people" defined by heritage (for example, English or French), instead grounding nationhood in a commitment to diversity and inclusion.[40] In this view, Canada is a country where shared progressive values, not shared history, religion, or culture, bind its citizens.

Of course, the notion that the United States and Canada are primarily propositional nations is philosophically untenable and historically inaccurate. Such claims are nothing more than a modern invention, traced to 20th-century secular progressives seeking to justify mass immigration as a means of solidifying their own cultural ascendancy and power. The facts, properly understood, point in the opposite direction.

What Actually Makes a Nation

Nations, by their very nature, require more than abstract principles to hold together; they depend on shared cultural, linguistic, and historical bonds that foster organic solidarity. As is becoming increasingly apparent, a country with no shared past lacks the loyalty to endure crises in the future. It's well known that native-born citizens with deep roots in their communities express stronger patriotism—they are a country's core defenders.[41] It should be obvious to our political leaders that transient newcomers—already lacking the loyalty of those ancestors who fought, farmed, and died on a nation's soil—will be even less invested in a country promoting itself as nothing more than "an idea." As promised, we will examine the research that explores this phenomenon more fully. For now, the insight of Aristotle provides a guiding framework.

The ancient Greek philosopher acknowledged that propositions—such as liberty and democracy—can inform governance, but they cannot replace the pre-political ties of kinship, custom, and shared memory that are essential to a stable society. Writing some 300 years before Christ, Aristotle emphasized that a common history and culture—not diversity—constitute a nation's strength. In *Politics,*

Book V, Chapter 3, he observed:

> Another cause of revolution is difference of ethnicities which do not at once acquire a common spirit; for a state is not the growth of a day, any more than it grows out of a multitude brought together by accident. Hence the reception of strangers in colonies, either at the time of their foundation or afterwards, has generally produced revolution.[42]

Philosophically, the propositional nation denies the social nature of humans. As Aristotle recognized long ago, nations are homes—organic communities shaped by history and habit—not ideological clubs.

Historically, the claim that either the U.S. or Canada was conceived as propositional nations falls flat. The political founders of both countries envisioned a nation where a specific people—with the exception of Quebec in Canada, a specific Anglo-Protestant people—would produce children to fill the land, maintaining in perpetuity their English language, Christian faith, and Western European culture. Moreover, the founding documents of both nations were expressions of inherited traditions, not the creation of new ideology.

The U.S. Declaration of Independence and Constitution drew directly from English legal and political traditions, including the Magna Carta, the Bill of Rights (1689), and centuries of common-law practice. The American founders saw themselves not as inventing new moral truths but as restoring rights they already possessed as Englishmen. Likewise, Canada's British North America Act (1867) was not a philosophical manifesto. It established a framework of parliamentary democracy, federalism, and the rule of law—all inherited from Britain.

There was no claim of founding a new nation based solely on abstract values like equality or liberty.

Early laws further reinforce that preservation of a specific cultural background was the goal of these early politicians. For example, the U.S. Naturalization Act of 1790 limited citizenship to free people of European origins of good moral character.[43] This wording highlights the political assumption that only people within a certain cultural and civilizational orbit could be guaranteed to integrate successfully.

The writings of America's early leaders make the point just as plainly. James Madison, often called the "Father of the Constitution" for his central role in drafting and promoting the U.S. Constitution and the Bill of Rights, emphasized the importance of a shared people in the nation's success. He wrote that "the kindred blood which flows in the veins of American citizens, the mingled blood which they have shed in defense of their sacred rights" is what consecrates the union of America.[44] In his writings on behalf of the American nation, Founding Father John Jay wrote:

> ... Providence has been pleased to give this one connected country to one united people—a people descended from the same ancestors, speaking the same language, professing the same religion, attached to the same principles of government, very similar in their manners and customs, and who, by their joint counsels, arms, and efforts, fighting side by side throughout a long and bloody war, have nobly established general liberty and independence.[45]

Likewise, early Canadian immigration policies favored settlers from

Britain and northern Europe, who were presumed uniquely able to assimilate into the Anglo-French cultural framework. In the 1865 Confederation Debates surrounding the creation of the nation of Canada, John A. MacDonald, who would go on to become the nation's first Prime Minister, explained:

> If we wish to be a great people; if we wish to form a great nationality, commanding the respect of the world, able to hold our own against all opponents, and to defend those institutions we prize; if we wish to have one system of government... [we must have] belonging, as they do, to the same nation, obeying the same Sovereign, owning the same allegiance, and being, for the most part, of the same blood and lineage...[46]

Later, as Prime Minister, in an 1885 speech on the country's immigration policies, MacDonald declared immigration for non-European countries should be discouraged. Instead, he said: "We want immigrants from the British Isles, from the United States, from Scandinavia, from Germany, from France, from Belgium, from Holland—in short, from the countries of Northern Europe."[47]

A Break with the Past

Such laws and statements from the early days of the United States and Canada make little sense if the nationhood of these countries were based purely on adherence to abstract propositions rather than shared heritage. However, in one respect, I believe these early laws and statements went too far. As clarified in the description of nationalism in Chapter 1, Traditional Conservatism today rejects the assertion (made by our earliest politicians) that the "same blood and lineage" is a prerequisite for citizenship and the status of a true countryman. Instead, "nationalism, as promoted by today's traditional conservatives, ignores race as a divide and seeks to include anyone of goodwill through cultural assimilation." It does so, however, with an important condition: prospective countrymen must, over an extended period of time, demonstrate commitment to their new nation "in language and cultural customs but also through steady contributions to the tax base, the strengthening of social cohesion, and the betterment of their communities."

Today's Traditional Conservatism makes this rejection of the "same blood and lineage" without contempt for these early architects of nationhood. It's understood that when the founding statesmen of the U.S. and Canada made such declarations, they were attempting to apply a worthwhile principle but in the absence of adequate knowledge and modern advancements. In their historical context, they knew that civilizational success rested on cultural unity and continuity and assumed that the only way to secure that was by choosing newcomers by country of origin, which, at the time, meant by race. In their day, it was nearly impossible to think that someone coming from a non-Western nation might fully embody the values and norms derived from Christianity and the English common law tradition. In all probability, they would not have.

In the modern era, the conditions that once made these earlier assumptions plausible have changed dramatically. The rise of global communication, the internet, mass travel, and instant access to information has created new ways for people to absorb culture and form moral character beyond the boundaries of geography or ancestry. A person born in Nairobi, Manila, or Mumbai may never have set foot in the United States or Canada, yet through exposure to English-language media, Western-style education, a local Christian church, and shared online spaces, may come to embody the same habits of thought, moral assumptions, and civic virtues that once defined the Anglo-Protestant world. Conversely, many native-born North Americans now find themselves detached from those very values, having embraced cosmopolitan ideologies that reject the moral inheritance of the West.

Thus, while the founders' focus on shared culture and moral continuity remains essential, modern technology has broadened the ways such continuity can be sustained. Cultural kinship is no longer exclusively tied to blood or locality. While such deep, tangible ties remain of great importance and cannot be dismissed, *cultural kinship* can now also be nurtured through shared participation in a moral and intellectual tradition that circulates digitally and globally. For perhaps the first time in history, two people who look nothing alike and live continents apart can be very similar in character, conviction, and disposition. This reality affirms the Traditional Conservative view that what ultimately unites a nation is not race, but the internalization of the West's civilizational ideals lived out over extended time.

Where the Myth of a Propositional Nation Leads

A central consequence of viewing America and Canada primarily as propositional nations is an increased willingness to undermine one's own country. When allegiance to abstract principles such as maximal rights, freedom, and democratic access is extended—even to those who are not fellow countrymen—while allegiance to one's fellow citizens declines, priorities become distorted. Within this framework, opposition to the removal of criminal or illegal migrants residing in the country is easily rationalized. If shared history, heritage, and lineage are dismissed as irrelevant to nationhood, then immigrants who possess none of these traits—even those who enter illegally or commit crimes—can be treated as de facto citizens. Indeed, such migrants may even be regarded as more authentically American or Canadian than heritage citizens, since they often profess stronger allegiance to abstract ideals such as unlimited liberty and expansive democracy.

Of course, this heightened allegiance is frequently rooted in self-interest: only if unlimited liberty and expansive democracy are treated as supreme does the legitimacy of their deportation come into question. For progressive activists advocating on their behalf, protecting such migrants thus appears not merely compassionate, but as a defense of what they perceive to be the nation's core propositional values.

If this analysis is dismissed as an exaggeration of contemporary left-wing positions, one need only consider recent events in cities such as Minneapolis. There, in the first months of 2026, progressive activists worked to block federal law-enforcement efforts to arrest and deport illegal immigrants, many with violent criminal records.[48] Valuing their extreme propositional positions more than their fellow countrymen, they portrayed enforcement itself as a moral wrong rather than a basic duty of government.

This dynamic is further illustrated by recent actions of left-leaning activists in several other American cities. In places such as Chicago, Los Angeles, and New Orleans, protesters have physically intervened to obstruct Immigration and Customs Enforcement (ICE) agents during deportation operations. They have formed human chains, thrown objects, assaulted officers, set vehicles on fire, and used community alerts and patrols to disrupt enforcement efforts. These actions have reportedly coincided with a 1150% surge in assaults on ICE personne l.[49]

In keeping with these radical notions of nationhood, this behavior is accompanied by appeals to universal human rights, chants portraying resistance as "what democracy looks like," and claims that protecting illegal migrants fulfills constitutional promises to all persons under shared values of acceptance, compassion, and openness.[50] In this way, these citizens act out their convictions about a propositional nation: by defining America solely in terms of abstract ideals of liberty and inclusion—rather than borders, law, or shared heritage—they treat undocumented migrants as embodiments of the nation's true essence. As a result, even violent or obstructive efforts to protect their presence are framed as moral acts undertaken in the service of preserving the country's ideological core over its legal or sovereign integrity. A similar expression of this propositional view of nationhood can be seen in Canada—not through private citizens interfering with government enforcement, but through the government's own policies effectively undermining the safety and interests of its private citizens.

From 2025 into 2026, in British Columbia's Surrey and Lower Mainland, a wave of violent extortion operations—including shootings, firebombings, and death threats—was linked to young Indian nationals who had entered the country on student visas and then remained illegally. When the Canada Border Services Agency initiated deportation proceedings against fifteen of these individuals, they immediately filed refugee claims, which automatically halted their removals under Canadian law. As a result, they were permitted to remain in the country—some on bail, others in detention—while their claims moved through a backlogged refugee system that can take years to resolve. During this period, those released on bail gained access to work permits, taxpayer-funded health care, and in some cases social assistance.[51]

The outcomes these foreign nationals received despite their serious offenses illustrate how Canada's courts and governing institutions have been realigned to embody and enforce the radical ideal of a "propositional nation." In a country grounded in traditional distinctions between citizens and non-citizens—and in corresponding notions of rights, obligations, and borders—we would have seen swift detention followed by prompt removal, with refugee claims barred in cases involving violent criminal activity. Instead, procedural mechanisms designed to protect abstract rights—rather than the interests of native citizens—were activated to suspend enforcement altogether.

For their part, these individuals did precisely what the theory of propositional nationhood suggests should be sufficient: they entered Canada, navigated its legal system, and, when faced with removal, invoked the very propositions the country claims to be built upon—unfettered liberty, expansive democracy, supplemented by multiculturalism, minority protections, and a universal right to asylum. Tellingly, for all the opportunity that was granted to them, none of it produced even minimal loyalty to Canada or its people; instead, the moment the legal shield of "refugee claimant" status was available, they weaponized Canada's own universalist propositions against itself.

In Canada, propositional principles have become the loophole; the more ruthlessly universalist the proposition is, the more easily a determined outsider can turn it into a one-way ratchet that protects him while he victimizes the citizens of the country. The BC case is therefore a lived refutation: when the nation is defined only by abstract propositions rather than by a people with common culture and shared history, those propositions can be gamed indefinitely by newcomers who feel no ancestral tie, no gratitude, and no communal obligation. We are left with a situation where the historic nation finances, medicates, and legally shields the very criminals who shoot up its citizens' businesses, all because the system is no longer allowed to ask, "who are our people?" and act accordingly.

The Lie: "We've Always Been a Nation of Immigrants"

To secure citizens' consent to the devaluation of their own citizenship, it must first be made to seem unimportant. As shown above, this is accomplished in part through the myth of the propositional nation. That myth, however, is further sustained by a powerful falsehood that erases the idea of national particularity altogether. Specifically, it is claimed—incorrectly—that the United States and Canada were never nations of distinct peoples, but merely perpetual projects of unending, diverse immigration.

Across North America, progressives in the highest offices of the land frequently insist "we've always been a nation of immigrants" whenever they are challenged on the merits of importing mass immigration from countries with dissimilar cultures.

While in office, Democratic President Barack Obama repeatedly affirmed this narrative. For example, in 2014, when advocating for legislation allowing five million illegal immigrants to avoid deportation, he pleaded for his fellow Americans' support, claiming, "America is and always has been a nation of immigrants."[52] As President, Obama's former running mate, Joe Biden, carried the refrain forward. For instance, in a 2024 speech celebrating Hispanic Heritage Month, he claimed: "We're a nation of immigrants. Since our founding, the very idea of America has been nurtured, enriched, and advanced by the contributions and sacrifices of immigrants."[53]

Singing from the same progressive hymnbook, Canadian Liberal Prime Minister Justin Trudeau never missed an opportunity to deny historical reality by suggesting that immigration from diverse cultures was responsible for most of Canada's history, growth, and success. In a 2017 speech celebrating Canada's 150th anniversary, he stated: "We are a country built on different cultures, different religions, different languages all coming together."[54] Shortly after, and in open defiance of sociological evidence, he went even further, claiming that immigrants possess a deeper connection to the country than native-born Canadians. He declared that newcomers have a greater right to Canada, insisting, "This is your country more than it is for others because we [native Canadians] take it for granted."[55]

It's simply not true that America and Canada were founded by immigrants. Such a claim reveals a significant definitional error and a misunderstanding of historical sequence.

The untamed, undeveloped territories of North America were founded by *settlers* from Europe, not immigrants. While Indigenous peoples inhabited the land long before European arrival, most lived in decentralized or semi-nomadic societies without the permanent settlements, written laws, or defined borders characteristic of European nationhood. The modern label "First Nations" is a retrospective political term, not a historical one, and applying it to pre-colonial indigenous societies alters the meaning of nationhood.

More to the point, the distinction between settlers and immigrants is essential for understanding how nations are formed, who defines their identity, and how cultural continuity is maintained. Though often conflated in modern discourse, the two play fundamentally different roles in the life of a country. Settlers are not simply early immigrants; they are the builders of nations. They establish the political, cultural, and institutional frameworks that later generations sustain and develop. Nations are born when a distinct people create a durable system of governance alongside a shared culture, and it is settlers—not immigrants—who perform this foundational work. In doing so, they shape a country's cultural DNA: its language, legal system, religion, moral code, and civic identity.

Immigrants, by contrast, are those who enter an already established nation-state, benefiting from the systems and traditions that settlers created but having no part in their original formation. Their arrival presupposes a functioning political order, stable economy, and coherent cultural identity—all of which have already been created by the settler population. Immigration is therefore an act of entry into an existing civilization, not its genesis. The role of the immigrant, ideally, is one of integration: to adopt the core values, language, and customs of the host society while contributing to its ongoing prosperity. To confuse this with the act of settlement is to misunderstand the historical sequence of nation-building.

Because settlers built the institutions and cultural order of a nation, they hold a unique historical claim to its identity. As has been repeatedly clarified, this does not mean that immigrants cannot become full citizens or valued members of society, but it does mean that citizenship alone does not erase the cultural lineage and ownership that flow from a nation's founding stock. When modern ideologies claim that all residents, regardless of origin, equally define a nation's identity, they disregard the reality that cultural inheritance is not instantly transferable.

To recognize the difference between settlers and immigrants is not to deny the value of immigration, but to restore historical clarity. Settlers create the framework of nationhood; immigrants join and, if they assimilate, enrich it. When these roles are confused, a society risks erasing the very cultural foundation that makes its existence possible. A healthy nation welcomes newcomers, but it does so on its own terms and with the understanding that what they are joining is not a blank slate—it's a living inheritance built by those who came first. Settlers set the rules of society; immigrants are meant to follow them.

The (Immigration) Numbers Don't Lie

Further exposing the falsehood that "America and Canada have always been nations of immigrants," it's also untrue that immigration became the main driver of growth after their founding. The fact is that once the first generations of settlers had carved civilization from the wilderness, population and progress were sustained largely by their own descendants rather than by new arrivals.

That is, throughout the 1800s and into the mid-1900s, it was primarily the high birthrates of these original settlers and their offspring that fueled population growth and preserved the cultural, linguistic, and institutional character of the new nations. Furthermore, until the 1960s, immigration from non-European countries to North America played virtually no role at all; the limited influx of newcomers that did occur came mostly from the same countries as the original settlers. The actual statistics bear this out.

From 1776 to 1860, almost 90% of America's population growth came from natural increase, with native-born families typically having five to seven children. After the Civil War, between 1860 and 1890, about 70% of growth was still from births, with the rest coming from immigrants, almost all from Northern Europe.

Between 1890 and 1920, births accounted for roughly 60% of population growth, while 40% came from immigration, which now included more people from Southern and Eastern Europe. In a fascinating rebound aided by strict immigration control, from 1920 to 1960 about 90% of growth again came from births alone.[56] Clearly, until the 1960s—when a new mindset favoring mass immigration took hold—America's growth was driven mainly by the children of its original European-descended population, not by immigrants. Canada's pattern of population growth basically mirrors that of the U.S. From the 1760s to the 1860s, nearly 90% of Canada's population growth came from natural increase, with native-born families typically having five to seven children. After Confederation in 1867 up to 1890, about 70% of growth still came from births, while the remaining immigrants arrived mostly from Northern Europe, especially the British Isles.

Between 1890 and 1920, births accounted for roughly 60% of population growth, with immigration increasing and drawing more people from other parts of Europe. With immigration restricted during the Great Depression and World Wars, from 1920 to 1960, about 90% of growth once again came from natural increase.[57]

Therefore, for most of its existence, Canada, like the U.S., has been a nation of settlers' offspring with a sprinkling of newcomers from Europe—not a nation of immigrants.

Is It Time to Remember?

Historically, the strongest challenge to the claim that the United States and Canada have always been nations of immigrants comes not from the distant past but from the period between 1920 and 1960. As just noted, during those decades in the modern era, both countries largely closed their doors to newcomers.

In the United States, the Immigration Act of 1924—also known as the Johnson-Reed Act or the National Origins Act—effectively ended immigration from Eastern and Southern Europe, as well as from other continents. Immigration was largely limited to individuals from Western Europe, Canada, and, to a lesser extent, Mexico. Even then, strict quotas were imposed, capping arrivals at no more than 150,000 newcomers per year—down from more than 1 million annually before the act was passed.

The act was a response to widespread public sentiment and received strong bipartisan support. As in today's debates, mass immigration was disrupting the labor market, as foreign workers accepted lower wages, undermining job opportunities and wages for native-born Americans. Also similar to today, economic concerns were matched by worries about cultural preservation. Many Americans—particularly those descended from earlier settlers—were witnessing firsthand rapid and unsettling changes in their communities as newcomers with different norms and values flooded in. In both implicit and explicit ways, the new arrivals were reshaping what had, until then, been understood as the country's foundational identity.

Concerns about national security also strengthened calls to halt immigration. From the early 1900s through the 1920s, communists, socialists, anarchists, and other political radicals were plentiful among the foreigners entering the United States. Their presence drew particular attention because of their highly visible efforts to establish groups and recruit supporters from among the native-born population.

The vast majority of Americans regarded the Johnson-Reed Act as essential for economic recovery and cultural survival. They believed that only by reducing immigration from a fire hose to a garden hose could the millions who had already poured into the country be given time to disperse beyond dense urban ethnic enclaves and gradually assimilate into the broader national culture.

But, as we have seen, collective memory is short, and in the absence of a visible threat, people will welcome ideas that earlier generations would have rejected outright.

In 1965, America's restrictive immigration framework established by the Johnson-Reed Act was replaced by the Hart-Celler Act, also known as the Immigration and Nationality Act of 1965. This law abolished the national-origins quota system created in the 1920s, thereby opening immigration to applicants from all regions of the world. It also introduced a new preference-based system that prioritized family reunification. Under this structure, one immigrant could sponsor multiple relatives—such as parents and siblings, who could in turn sponsor their own immediate family members—contributing to substantial increases over time. By the early 2000s, legal immigration to the United States averaged more than one million arrivals per year.

The Democratic lawmakers who drafted the Hart-Celler Act, together with their progressive allies, presented its provisions as essential to advancing social justice and civil rights. Key among those allies were the American Jewish Committee and the American Jewish Congress, who argued that a society marked by greater ethnic and religious diversity would make it more difficult for large, organized antisemitic movements to gain political traction.[58] By contrast, the principles underlying the earlier Johnson-Reed Act were portrayed as narrow, discriminatory, and out of step with modern values.

For a fuller understanding of the case made by supporters of Hart-Celler, return to Chapter 6 and review the sections discussing the ideas associated with the Post-War Consensus. In brief, the overarching messaging was this: pluralism and diversity are the highest goods; they alone can prevent a nation from slipping into authoritarianism.

In Canada, the political trajectory closely paralleled that of the United States. Between 1910 and 1923, Parliament passed a series of measures designed to tighten, not relax, eligibility for legal residence. The last major restrictive statute before the 1960s was the Immigration Act of 1952, which reinforced preferences for immigrants from the United Kingdom, Ireland, France, the United States, and selected Commonwealth countries.

Canada's shift away from strict immigration controls began around 1962. Unlike the United States, this change did not occur through a single sweeping statute but through regulatory reforms enacted by orders-in-council—an approach made possible by Canada's parliamentary system, which allows the executive to act without the same level of legislative debate required in the U.S. The easing of restrictions was driven by many of the same forces seen south of the border, including civil rights advocacy, ethnic lobbying, and postwar commitments to pluralism.

As argued earlier in this chapter, certain elements of pre-1960s immigration policy in the United States and Canada went beyond good-faith efforts to preserve cultural continuity and crossed into racial prejudice. In many cases, these decisions were shaped less by animosity toward other ethnic groups than by a worldview conditioned by its own historical context and limitations. Even so, when policy moves from cultural prudence into racial discrimination, that line has been crossed—and traditional conservatives, myself included, reject such reasoning outright.

With those caveats in place, however, there remains a lesson to be drawn from legislation such as the Johnson-Reed Act. In both the United States and Canada today, we face circumstances that resemble those confronting native-born North Americans in the early twentieth century. Collective memory may fade, but a visible threat can quickly revive it—reminding us that earlier generations acted decisively when they believed their nations' long-term stability and character were at stake.

Endnotes for Chapter 2

1. Gallup, "Immigration Surges to Top of Most Important Problem List," March 26, 2025, https://news.gallup.com/poll/611135/immigration-surges-top-important-problem-list.aspx; Abacus Data, "1 in 2 Canadians Say Immigration Is Harming the Nation, Up 10 Points Since Last Year," October 18, 2024, https://abacusdata.ca/1-in-2-canadians-say-immigration-is-harming-the-nation/.

2. For example, Brian C. Joondeph, "Why the Babies (and the Voters) Might Be Moving Right," *American Thinker*, November 16, 2025, https://www.americanthinker.com/articles/2025/11/why_the_babies_and_the_voters_might_be_moving_right.html.

3. Simone Moriconi, Giovanni Peri, and Riccardo Turati, "Are Immigrants More Left-Leaning than Natives?" NBER Working Paper No. 30523 (Cambridge, MA: National Bureau of Economic Research, October 2022), 1–5, https://doi.org/10.3386/w30523.

4. Augustine, *The City of God*, Book 1, Chapter 17, 33, trans. Henry Bettenson (London: Penguin Books, 1972).

5. Thomas Aquinas, *Summa Theologica*, II-II, Q. 26, A. 2, trans. Fathers of the English Dominican Province (New York: Benziger Bros., 1947).

6. Margaret Thatcher, interview by Brian Walden, *Weekend World*, London Weekend Television, January 6, 1980, In The Margaret Thatcher Foundation, "Transcript: ... Good Samaritan ... ," https://archive.margaretthatcher.org/doc01/2193F2214D8E4842A573084E7DFCEB16. pdf

7. Josh Boak, "What is 'Ordo Amoris?' Vice President JD Vance Invokes This Medieval Catholic Concept," *AP News*, February 6, 2025, https://apnews. com/article/jd-vance-catholic-theology-migration-e868af574fb2e742c6ed3d 756c569769.

8. For example, Jonah McKeown, "What Is the 'Ordo Amoris'? JD Vance's Comments on Christian Love Spark Debate," *Catholic News Agency*, May 30, 2025, https://www.catholicnewsagency.com/news/261989/what-is-the-ordo-amoris-jd-vances-comments-on-christian-love-spark-debate.

9. See Russell K. Nieli, *Wounds That Will Not Heal: Affirmative Action and Our Continuing Racial Divide* (New York: Encounter Books, 2012).

10. For example, Laura Giuliano, David I. Levine, and Jonathan Leonard, "Manager Race and the Race of New Hires," *Journal of Labor Economics* 27, no. 4 (2009): 589–631, https://doi.org/10.1086/605946.

11. Nieli, *Wounds That Will Not Heal*, 117.

12. Gad Saad, *Suicidal Empathy: The Psychotic Logic of Globalism* (Washington, DC: Regnery Publishing, 2025).

13. See Yossi Hasson et al., "Are Liberals and Conservatives Equally Motivated to Feel Empathy Toward Others?," *Personality and Social Psychology Bulletin* 44, no. 10 (2018): 1449–59, https://doi.org/10.1177/0146167218769867; and David Sparkman, Scott Eidelman, and Derrick F. Till, "Ingroup and Outgroup Interconnectedness Predict and Promote Political Ideology Through Empathy," *Group Processes & Intergroup Relations* 22, no. 8 (2019): 1161–80, https://doi.org/10.1177/1368430218819794.

14. Adam Waytz et al., "Ideological Differences in the Expanse of the Moral Circle," *Nature Communications* 10, no. 1 (2019): 4389, https://doi. org/10.1038/s41467-019-12227-0.

15. Ibid.

16. Christopher A. Simon, Nicholas P. Lovrich, Kristina G. Verboncoeur, and Matthew C. Moltz, "Re-examining Willingness to Fight for One's Country: Exploring Nature of Conflict and Citizenship Status Effects in the United States and Canada," *Armed Forces & Society* (2024), https:// doi.org/ 10.1177/0095327X241269905. For Canada also see Angus Reid Institute, "Half Say They'd Go to War for Canada, but Young People Far Less Willing to Enlist," *Angus Reid Institute*, July 9, 2025, https://angusreid. org/canada-volunteer-military-service/. Note that NDP voters stand as a proxy

for the most progressive citizens in Canada.

17. Ibid.

18. "Most Racist Countries 2025," *World Population Review*, https:// worldpopulationreview.com/country-rankings/most-racist-countries.

19. Ibid.

20. For example: David North, "H-1B Developments: One Firm Pays for Anti-White Hiring Practices, Another Sued for Anti-Untouchable," *Center for Immigration Studies*, July 14, 2020, https://cis.org/North/H1B-Developments-One-Firm-Pays-AntiWhite-Hiring-Practices-Another-Sued-AntiUntouchable; David North, "H-1B Hiring: Bias within Bias, Discrimination within Discrimination," *Center for Immigration Studies*, February 10, 2017, https://cis.org/North/H1B-Hiring-Bias-within-Bias-Discrimination-within-Discrimination; Matina Stevis-Gridneff, "Canada Tightens Immigration Policy And Leaves Thousands in Limbo," *New York Times*, October 12, 2024, https://www.nytimes.com/2024/10/12/world/canada/canada-immigration-policy.html.

21. Eric Fan and Coulter Jones, "IT Outsourcer Gamed US H-1B Visa Lottery for Indian Workers Over Others," *Bloomberg*, December 9, 2024, https://www. bloomberg.com/graphics/2024-cognizant-h1b-visas-discriminates-us-workers/.

22. U.S. Citizenship and Immigration Services, *H-1B Petitions by Beneficiary Country of Birth and Employer State, Fiscal Year 2024* (Washington, DC: U.S. Department of Homeland Security, 2025), Table 3, https://www.uscis.gov / sites/default/files/document/reports/FY2024_H-1B_Petitions_by_Country_ of_Birth_and_Employer_State.pdf.

23. Kurtis Lee and Marcelo Rochabrun, "Indian Firms Gamed H-1B Visa Lottery, U.S. Says, Costing Americans Jobs," *Bloomberg*, June 12, 2024, https://www. bloomberg.com/graphics/2024-indian-companies-h1b-visa-lottery-fraud/; Ron Hira, *The Offshore Outsourcing of High-Skilled Jobs: H-1B Visas and the Wage Suppression Effect* (Washington, DC: Economic Policy Institute, February 2021), 18–22, https://www.epi.org/publication/offshoring-h1b-visas-2021/; U.S. Attorney's - Office, Eastern District of California, "Indian National Pleads Guilty to H-1B Visa Fraud Scheme Involving Over 3,000 Fake Registrations," news release, September 18, 2024, https://www.justice. gov/usao-edca/pr/indian-national-pleads-guilty-h-1b-visa-fraud-scheme.

24. Internal Revenue Service, *Publication 519: U.S. Tax Guide for Aliens* (Washington, DC: IRS, 2024), https://www.irs.gov/publications/p519#en_ US_2024_publink1000222500.

25. Ibid.

26. See Douglas Todd, "Little-Known Program Dominates Canada's Massive Guest-Worker Scheme," *Vancouver Sun*, September 12, 2024, https://vancouver-

sun. com/opinion/columnists/little-known-program-domi-nates-canadas-massive-guest-worker-scheme.

27. For example, Marie Woolf, "Ottawa Urged to Clamp Down Further on Immigration Employment Scam," *The Globe and Mail*, September 29, 2023, https://www.theglobeandmail.com/amp/politics/article-ott awa-urged-to-clamp-down-further-on-immigration-employ ment-scam/.

28. This article purports to correct misleading information on the wage subsidies while it in fact provides damning information about them: Marissa Birnie, "Claims About Wage Subsidies for Immigrants and Temporary Workers in Canada Are Misleading," *The Canadian Press*, June 27, 2025, https://www.thecanadianpressnews.ca/fact_checking/claim s-about-wage-subsidies-for-immigrants-and-temporary-wor kers-in-canada-are-misleading/ article_4248f77b-1ff6-5a6d-b865-dc458a8eac40.html.

29. For example, Lygia Navarro, "The Night Watchmen," *The Local*, December 16, 2022, https://thelocal.to/security-gua rds-international-students-brampton/.

30. For example, "Indian-Origin Suspects Among 18 Arrested In Canada Towing Industry Scam," *NDTV*, June 17, 2025, https://www.ndtv.co m/ world-news/indian-origin-suspects-among-18-arrest ed-in-canada-towing-industry-scam-8689178.

31. For example, Rahim Mohamed, "Alberta minister calls on feds to crack down on foreign trucking scams," *National Post*, December 23, 2025, https://nationalpost.com/news/canada/alberta-minister-calls-on-feds-to-crack-down-on-foreign-trucking-scams.

32. Wiretap Media (@WiretapMedia), "This Tim Hortons in Grand Bend, Ontario just changed ownership. The new owners fired every single employee and replaced them with Indian foreign workers," *X*, October 30, 2025, https://x.com/WiretapMedia/status/1854529183746191624; Jason Lavigne, "Tim Hortons in Grand Bend Fires All Canadian Staff, Replaces with Indian TFWs—Locals Fight Back," *Substack (Lavigne Reports)*, November 2, 2025, https://jasonlavigne.substack.com/p/tim-hortons-grand-bend-fires-all; u/ GrandBendResident and subsequent thread, "Grand Bend Tim Hortons just fired all the local staff and replaced them with TFWs from India," *Reddit r/ LMIASCAMS*, October 31, 2025, https://www.reddit.com/r/LMIASCAMS/ comments/1gfq8z3/grand_bend_tim_hortons_just_fired_all_the_local/.

33. Tim Hortons (@TimHortons), "We have a Tim Hortons franchisee in Grimsby, Ontario . . . ," *X (formerly Twitter)*, December 18, 2025, 21:14 GMT, https://x.com/TimHortons/status/2001763030221115526; Dean Allison (@DeanAllisonMP), "Hey, @TimHortons, what are you doing in your @TownofGrimsby stores? . . . ," *X (formerly Twitter)*, December 18, 2025, 20:32 GMT, https://x.com/DeanAllisonMP/status/2001752498437018018; life-

withsonduren (@lifewitsonduren), "Tim Hortons fires nearly all Canadian staff @ 4 locations in Grimsby Ontario ," *X (formerly Twitter)*, December 18, 2025, 15:08 GMT, https://x.com/lifewitsonduren/ status/2001670820523921585.

34. Chris Knight, "Tim Hortons Workers Linked to Alleged Marriage Fraud Immigration Scheme," *National Post*, October 1, 2025, https://nationalpost. com/news/canada/picton-tim-hortons-marriage-fraud.

35. For example, Mario Nawfal (@MarioNawfal), "CANADIAN BUSINESS OWNER DROPS BOMBSHELL: GOV'T PAYS HIM TO HIRE MIGRANTS OVER LOCALS," *X (formerly Twitter)*, May 9, 2025, https://x. com/MarioNawfal/status/1920773236398145784; User Chemixrx, "Why Has Every Tim Hortons in My City Switched to Indian Staff Overnight?," *Reddit r/TimHortons*, October 2022, https://www.reddit.com/r/TimHortons/ comments/y74pjr/is_tim_hortons_sponsoring_indian_workers/.

36. For example, Ritu Singh, "Canadian Woman Alleges Discriminatory Practices at Tim Hortons: 'Only Hiring Indians,'" *NDTV*, October 3, 2024, https://www.ndtv.com/feature/canadian-woman-alleges-tim-hortons-only-hires-indians-claims-she-was-fired-for-speaking-out-6730080.

37. J-TV: The Global Jewish Channel, "Jordan Peterson STUNNED as Douglas Murray Reveals Why Islamic Countries Always Fail," *YouTube video*, 5:51, posted August 6,

2025, https://www.youtube.com/watch?v=UzyfVJ2v3xI.

38. National Archives, "Declaration of Independence: A Transcription," *National Archives*, https://www.archives.gov/founding-docs/declaration-transcript.

39. Abraham Lincoln Presidential Library and Museum, "Gettysburg Address," https://presidentlincoln.illinois.gov/exhibits/online-exhibits/gettysburg-address-everett-copy/.

40. For example, Keith Banting, "The Canadian Model of Integration: Multiculturalism and Social Cohesion," in *Immigration and Integration in Canada in the Twenty-First Century*, edited by John Biles, Meyer Burstein, and James Frideres (Montreal: McGill-Queen's University Press, 2008).

41. American National Election Studies, "2017 Pilot Study," (Ann Arbor, MI: University of Michigan, 2017), https://electionstudies.org/data-center/2017-pilot-study/; Pew Research Center, "The Generation Gap in American Politics," August 1, 2018, https://www.pewresearch.org/politics/2018/08/01/ the-generation-gap-in-american-politics/.

42. Aristotle, *Politics*, trans. Benjamin Jowett, https://classics.mit.edu/Aristotle/ politics.5.five.html.

43. Kunal M. Parker, *Making Foreigners: Immigration and Citizenship Law in America, 1600–2000* (Cambridge: Cambridge University Press, 2015), 75–77, https://doi.org/10.1017/CBO9781139343282.

44. Ben R. Crenshaw and Mike Sabo, "The Myth of the Propo-

sitional Nation," *American Reformer*, July 25, 2024, https
://americanreformer.org/2024/07/ the-myth-of-the-propo-
sitional-nation/.

45. Ibid.

46. John A. Macdonald, speech in the Legislative Assembly,
Province of Canada, February 6, 1865, in *Parliamentary Debates on the Subject of the Confederation of the British North
American Provinces* (Quebec: Hunter, Rose & Co., 1865),
transcription available at https://primarydocuments.ca/con
federation-debates-legislative-assembly-february-6-1865/.

47. Sir John A. Macdonald, speech in the House of Commons,
May 4, 1885, quoted in Joshua D. K. Mann, "The Bigots
Who Shaped Canada: John A. Macdonald," *An Injustice!*,
June 9, 2023, https://aninjusticemag.com/the-bigots-who
-shaped-a-canada-john-a-macdonald-b09ed12dca5e.

48. Emily Witt, "The Battle for Minneapolis: As Donald Trump
Brings His Retribution to a Liberal City, Citizens, Protesters,
and Civic Leaders Try to Protect One Another," *The New
Yorker*, January 25, 2026, https://www. newyorker.com/ne
ws/dispatch/the-battle-for-minneapolis.

49. U.S. Department of Homeland Security, "Sanctuary
Politicians' Rhetoric Fuels More Than 1,150% Increase in
Violence Against ICE Law Enforcement," news release,
November 24, 2025,
https://www.dhs.gov/news/2025/11/24/sanctuary-politicia
ns-rhetoric-fuels-more-1150-increase-violence-against-ice-law

50. For example, the National Immigration Law Center (NILC) provides a "Know Your Rights" guide emphasizing that immigrants have First Amendment protections to participate in protests against immigration enforcement, framing such participation as part of engaging in "our democracy" and exercising free speech rights guaranteed by the Constitution, National Immigration Law Center, "Know Your Rights: Immigrants' Participation in Protests," January 26, 2025, https://www.nilc.org/resources/ immigrant-participation-in-protests-rights/.

51. Stewart Bell, "Extortion Suspects Have Claimed Refugee Status, Canada's Border Agency Says," *Global News*, December 11, 2025 (updated December 14, 2025), https://globalnews.ca/news/11572311/extortion-suspects-claim-refugee-status-cbsa/.

52. Barack Obama, address to the nation on immigration, November 20, 2014, *The Guardian*, "Barack Obama's Speech on Immigration—Full Transcript," November 20, 2014, https://www.theguardian.com/us-news/2014/nov/20/obama-plan-shield-five-million-undocumented-migrants-deportation-speech.

53. Joseph R. Biden Jr., "Remarks by President Biden at a Reception Celebrating Hispanic Heritage Month and Honoring the Contributions of the Latino Community to the United States," *The White House*, September 18, 2024,

https://bidenwhitehouse.archives.gov/briefing-room/speec
hes-remarks/2024/09/18/remarks-by-president-biden-at-a-r
eception-celebrating-hispanic-heritage-month-and-honorin
g-the-contributions-of-the-latino-community-to-the-united
-states/.

54. Justin Trudeau, "Prime Minister Justin Trudeau's Address to the 72nd Session of the United Nations General Assembly," *Prime Minister of Canada*, September
21, 2017, https://www.pm.gc.ca/en/news/speeches/201
7/09/21/ prime-minister-justin-trudeaus-address-72th-ses-
sion-united-nations-general.

55. Rachel Gilmore, "Justin Trudeau 'jealous' of immigrants and
families who chose Canada," *Global News*, June 30, 2017,
https://globalnews.ca/ news/3567893/justin-trudeau-jeal-
ous-immigrants-ctv-interview/.

56. Michael R. Haines, "Fertility and Mortality in the United
States," *Economic   History   Association*,
https://eh.net/encyclopedia/fertility-and-mortality-in-the-u
nited-states/; "Immigration   to   the   United   States,
1851–1900,"   *Library   of   Congress*,
https://www.loc.gov/classroom-materials/united-states-hist
ory-primary-source-timeline/rise-of-industrial-america-1876
-1900/immigration-to-united-states-1851-1900/; Douglas
S. Massey, "A Brief History of U.S. Immigration Policy from
the Colonial Period to the Present Day," *Cato Institute Policy
Analysis*,   no.   919   (August   3,   2021),
https://www.cato.org/policy-analysis/brief-history-us-immi

gration-policy-colonial-period-present-day; National Academies of Sciences, Engineering, and Medicine, "2 Immigration to the United States: Current Trends in Historical Perspective," in *The Economic and Fiscal Consequences of Immigration* (Washington, DC: The National Academies Press, 2017), 77–140, https://nap.nationalacademies.org/read/23550/chapter/5.

57. Statistics Canada, "Population Growth: Migratory Increase Overtakes Natural Increase," https://www150.statcan.gc.ca/n1/pub/11-630-x/11-630-x2014001-eng.htm; James Belich et al., eds., "1.2 Historical Demography of Canada, 1608–1921," in *Canadian History: Post-Confederation*, BCcampus, https:// opentextbc.ca/postconfederation/chapter/1-2-historical-demography-of-canada-1608-1921/; John Douglas Belshaw, "10.2 Demographics," in *Canadian History: Pre-Confederation*, BCcampus, https://opentextbc.ca/preconfederation/ chapter/10-2-demographics/.

58. Stuart Svonkin, *Jews Against Prejudice: American Jews and the Fight for Civil Liberties* (New York: Columbia University Press, 1997), 34; Giovanni Facchini, Timothy J. Hatton, and Max F. Steinhardt, "Opening Heaven's Door: Public Opinion and Congressional Votes on the 1965 Immigration Act," *IZA Discussion Paper No. 14934* (Bonn: Institute of Labor Economics, 2021); Jerry Kammer, "The Hart-Celler Immigration Act of 1965: Political Figures and Historic Circumstances Produced Dramatic, Unintended Consequences" (Washington, DC: Center for Immigration Studies, October 2015); Otis L. Graham Jr., "A Vast So-

cial Experiment: The Immigration Act of 1965," *NPG Forum* (Arlington, VA: Negative Population Growth, October 2005); Maddalena Marinari, "Divided and Conquered: Immigration Reform Advocates and the Passage of the 1952 Immigration and Nationality Act," *Journal of American Ethnic History* 35, no. 3 (Spring 2016): 9–40; Raffi Wineburg, "From the Archive: Jews Welcome the Stranger," *Jewish Telegraphic Agency*, November 30, 2014, https://www.jta. org/2014/11/30/archive/from-the-archive-jews-welcome-the-stranger.

3

Sameness Is Our Strength: Why Diversity Divides

Diversity Weakens Society

The myth of the propositional nation—supported by the lie that the U.S. and Canada have always been mere collections of diverse immigrants—has led many to believe the progressive narrative that citizenship is nothing more than a trifle to be handed to anyone who wants it. But the progressive narrative does not end with the devaluation of citizenship. Once citizenship has been stripped of meaning, the next step is to glorify and exaggerate the supposed benefits of immigration, even mass immigration. This exaggeration is captured in the endlessly repeated slogan, "diversity is our strength."

In this slogan, *diversity* is not just a simple fact of population variety but a deliberate political and moral agenda. It's the promotion and elevation of groups, identities, and perspectives that differ from the majority population, often at the expense of the majority population. Race, ethnicity, religion, language, gender, and sexual orientation are all spotlighted, with the implicit—and often explicit—claim that the inclusion and empowerment of minority groups inherently "strengthen" or improve society by providing moral, cultural, and economic advantages.

Progressive politicians, educators, and media figures who endlessly repeat that "diversity is our strength" want to signal moral virtue, justify mass immigration, and redefine national identity around pluralism rather than shared culture or history. Difference is framed as singularly valuable while the majority's traditions, cohesion, and norms are cast as obstacles to justice and moral progress. Yet decades of research tell a far different story: greater diversity—in particular, cultural diversity—equals greater societal decline.

Ironically, the "discovery" that diversity—as promoted by progressives—is ruinous for society came about when one of the world's most elite researchers was trying to prove its benefits. In the early 2000s, Harvard sociologist Robert Putnam conducted over 30 thousand interviews across America as part of the largest study on civic engagement in history.[1] A self-described liberal and strong supporter of diversity, Putnam was distressed to find that virtually every measure of civic health was lower where ethnic diversity was higher. In fact, charity, volunteering, friendships with neighbors, membership in community organizations, and feelings of personal safety and security of property all suffered in proportion to increased racial, cultural, and religious differences.[2] Like a typical progressive academic faced with uncomfortable truths, he tried to spin a more politically correct narrative for the public—something that could save the reputation of diversity. Even though his data were ready in 2000, he admitted to putting off official publication, spending years trying to find other explanations. But the connection between diversity and societal unraveling remained consistent and strong.[3]

When he finally published a detailed scholarly analysis in June 2007 in the relatively obscure journal *Scandinavian Political Studies*, he couldn't let the data speak for themselves. Determined to convince the public that diversity was still a strength, he transformed his scholarly work into a vehicle for advocacy.[4] As one commentator noted, "Having aligned himself with the central planners [Marxists] intent on sustaining such social engineering, Putnam concludes the [uncomfortable] facts with a stern pep talk."[5] In this "pep talk," he argued that the negative effects of diversity he had discovered could be overcome and suggested that the challenges posed by diversity might eventually fade over time.[6]

Yet Putnam's final editorial comments about unity being just over the horizon stood in direct contrast to the hard data presented in the body of his paper. His analysis specifically tested the core claim of *contact theory*—the idea that contact with people from different ethnic backgrounds over time leads to greater understanding and harmony. His findings unequivocally rejected that proposition.[7]

Since the publication of Putnam's findings, there have been persistent and often desperate attempts to disprove them. (The researchers' desperation is evident in their attempts to frame their findings as temporary or subject to change, and to spin the data as "good news" by pointing out that, in segregated enclaves where a particular ethnic minority dominates, members of *that* group feel *mostly* comfortable.) Yet the overwhelming evidence continues to confirm Putnam's conclusions.

For instance, about a decade after his publication, a meta-analysis of 90 studies—each examining the effects of ethnic diversity on social cohesion—consistently supported his results.[8] Among other variables, the report, published in the *Annual Review of Sociology*, focused on evidence for the "constriction claim." At its heart, this claim hypothesizes that ethnic diversity leads to a broad retreat—or constriction—from social life, affecting not just interactions between different ethnic groups but also within the same ethnic group. Putnam famously described this "constriction" as people "hunkering down" like a turtle—pulling into their shells and disengaging from community involvement.[9] The authors of the meta-analysis stated that "Across all countries, we found strong support for the constriction claim," with a significant negative impact on localized interactions and attitudes, such as trusting, helping, or cooperating with neighbors, spending time socializing with neighbors, or engaging in informal neighborhood-based activities.[10] Interestingly, the meta-analysis found that the effects, felt across the West, were most profound and consistent in the United States.[11] There is a specific reason that ethnic diversity has the most damaging effect on social cohesion in the United States. Unlike countries such as France, Germany, or Canada, the U.S. government has never adopted multiculturalism as official policy. Instead, America embraced the "melting pot" model, which expects immigrants to abandon their native ethnicity—their previous customs, languages, and values—in order to merge into a single national culture. This ideal of assimilation is deeply tied to the American sense of identity.

Consequently, when immigrant groups fail—or are perceived as failing—to assimilate, the response from the majority population is often more severe, as non-assimilation is seen not just as cultural difference but as a rejection of the national ideal itself. For this reason, ethnic diversity in the United States tends to provoke stronger feelings of division and distrust than in societies where multiculturalism has been actively promoted as government policy.[12] That said, across the West, there is no country where greater diversity *positively* affects social cohesion.

Mores, Not Melanin, Drive Distrust

This American phenomenon—the greater negative impact of ethnic diversity here—provides an important lesson. It shows that declines in social trust and civic engagement are driven by more than mere exposure to people of different skin colors. Put another way, the meta-analysis found that cultural, not racial, differences made Americans the most uneasy. More recent studies, while continuing to corroborate Putnam's original findings, also demonstrate—through an untangling of the variables—that cultural differences have a bigger impact on trust and civic life than visible racial differences do.[13]

Of particular importance to this advancement in clarity was a landmark study published in 2020 in the *Annual Review of Political Science*.[14] The authors conducted a comprehensive meta-analysis of 87 studies, encompassing over 1,000 estimates, to examine how ethnic diversity affects social trust. They analyzed trust in different contexts—including trust in strangers, neighbors, co-ethnics, and out-groups—and considered a broad definition of ethnic diversity encompassing customs, values, language, religion, nationality, and traits such as skin color. The goal was to determine whether specific aspects of diversity, particularly cultural elements, explained the negative effects often attributed to ethnic diversity as a whole.[15]

The conclusion was clear: Differences in customs, values, and language explain the drop in trust much more than skin color or visible racial differences do. For example, language barriers predicted lower trust more strongly than race did in 65% of the studies, and differences in core values were the main reason for the negative effects in 22 out of 30 studies. Skin color can correlate with cultural differences, but it's primarily the mores of a group, not their melanin, that drives the decline in trust.[16]

This all makes implicit sense to traditional conservatives. For them, it's common sense that all cultures are *not* equal; they maintain that cultures shaped by Christian norms and values produce better outcomes. Therefore, when studies indicate that the introduction of non-Western customs and values into Western societies is associated with declines in social cohesion, they are not surprised. They expect that native citizens will feel unsettled when large numbers of newcomers arrive promoting beliefs and practices at odds with those that have historically strengthened their nation. For traditional conservatives, this reaction is not a matter of bigotry but a conclusion supported by empirical evidence.

To support the traditional conservative contention that the norms and values of non-Western nations are *less* conducive to social cohesion, I will not reiterate the unique benefits enjoyed by nations founded on Christianity, which fill the pages of earlier chapters. Rather, I'll briefly highlight a few recent sociological studies that directly compare trust across different cultural backgrounds.

Social Trust Across Nations

In a large-scale study, the School of Economics at the University of East Anglia in Britain recruited roughly 1,500 participants from 15 countries, including Western nations such as Denmark, Switzerland, the UK, and the U.S., and non-Western countries such as China, Japan, South Korea, and India.[17] The research used two experiments to measure dishonesty. The first was a coin-flip task: participants privately flipped a coin and reported the outcome, receiving a higher monetary reward for reporting "heads." Since the true probability is 50%, any aggregate result above that level indicated dishonesty.

The second experiment was a quiz task in which participants answered six music trivia questions without looking up answers online, earning a monetary reward for answering all correctly. Three questions were designed to be impossible without cheating, so correct answers on these indicated dishonest behavior. While dishonesty was detected in all countries in both tasks, the levels varied significantly (chiefly on the coin flip) with participants from Western nations—particularly those associated with Protestant Christianity—having the lowest levels of dishonesty, while those from China, India, and other Asian countries showed the highest levels.[18]

In a different experiment, detailed in the journal *Science*, researchers tested honesty by placing more than 17,000 "lost" wallets in 355 cities across 40 countries.[19] Through rigorous statistical analysis, they determined that the institutional and cultural variables dominant in Western nations—such as strong rule-of-law traditions and moral norms extending beyond close kinship or in-group ties—are positively associated with higher wallet-return rates. Conversely, in countries where citizens perceive corruption to be a fact of daily life and institutional trust is low—in the study, China and certain Muslim-majority countries stood out for this—dishonesty at the individual level is more prevalent.[20]

Despite the denials of progressives everywhere, it's not unreasonable to assume that immigrants coming from low-trust societies where dishonesty and corruption are expected will bring the habits of their homeland to their new country. In fact, we need not assume, as the research bears this out. Immigrants coming from both high-trust societies and low-trust societies pass along their attitudes and behaviors to their children, even to the second and third generations.[21] For instance, immigrants and their descendants from high-trust European countries like Sweden or Norway exhibit higher trust than those from low-trust origins like China or India, even after controlling for socioeconomic factors.[22]

Those with low trust levels demonstrate this characteristic in society by participating less in cooperative activities, depending more on detailed contracts or close monitoring to ensure obligations are met, and investing less in education, entrepreneurial ventures, and effective civic institutions. They also shy away from building diverse networks that would enhance economic and social prosperity.[23]

When "Trust No One" is the Best Advice

Extending these facts to everyday life, it follows that citizens of the West, raised in high-trust cultures where honesty is expected, may face a new type of threat because of mass immigration from low-trust countries. They may be unprepared for more frequent deception and, as a result, become easy prey. On one level, this challenge to civic trust is captured in increasing news reports of Chinese students at American and Canadian universities being disproportionately caught cheating.[24] A further blow to civic trust came in early 2026, when reports revealed that tens of thousands of Indian immigrants in Western countries were obtaining professional positions using fake degrees illegally purchased in their home country. In Australia alone, government officials disclosed that between 2025 and 2026, more than 23,000 workers from India were found to have secured employment with fraudulent credentials, many in critical sectors such as health care and child education.[25]

A more glaring example of foreign nationals preying on trusting North Americans is the surge in telephone and online scams targeting senior citizens. The FBI reported losses from Indian-run operations that exceeded $10 billion in 2023 and $5 billion from Chinese syndicates.[26] In 2024, five Chinese nationals were indicted in San Diego for a $27 million government impersonation scam hitting over 2,000 seniors.[27] In 2025, a team of Indian nationals operating out of Ohio was convicted of defrauding elderly Americans in four states of their life savings.[28] The massive work-visa scams and discriminatory hiring schemes perpetrated by India-based businessmen in North America, described in the previous chapter, are further examples of abuse of trust.

The largest U.S. fraud scheme was discovered in 2025 and involved Somali immigrants in Minnesota. Initially, it was estimated that the U.S. government had been bilked of about $1 billion in taxpayer funds, much of it siphoned through COVID-19 relief programs. Further investigation, however, uncovered even broader abuse. The largest branch of the scheme involved a nonprofit known as *Feeding Our Future*, which worked with the Minnesota Department of Education and the U.S. Department of Agriculture to provide meals to low-income children. Between 2019 and 2022, operators allegedly submitted fake invoices and inflated meal counts for food that was never delivered, stealing at least $250–300 million in federal funds. Federal prosecutors charged more than 78 people—almost exclusively first- and second-generation Somalis.[29]

Two other plots connected to the same general group pushed total losses past $1 billion. For example, the Housing Stabilization Services program, set up in 2020 to provide housing assistance to the disabled and the elderly, lost an estimated $302 million to bogus claims by fraudulent providers. A state autism therapy program was cheated out of nearly $220 million through inflated or fake services.[30]

By late 2025, federal prosecutors expanded investigations into 14 high-risk Medicaid-funded programs operating in Minnesota, estimating total fraud losses could reach $9 billion since 2018, with schemes involving overbilling, fabricated services, and kickbacks primarily within the Somali community.[31] Specific to daycare fraud, a viral video released in late December 2025 by conservative YouTuber Nick Shirley alleged that Somali-run child care centers in Minneapolis were fraudulently receiving millions from the Child Care Assistance Program without providing services, claiming sites appeared empty or inaccessible. In response, the Trump administration froze all federal childcare payments to Minnesota and imposed new verification requirements nationwide.[32]

Prosecutors say that, in many cases, the perpetrators used the proceeds of their crimes—meant for the state's most vulnerable citizens—to purchase luxury cars, tropical vacations, jewelry, and to pad overseas bank accounts.[33] Red flags appeared as early as 2019, but state officials reportedly did little follow-up amid relaxed pandemic rules and pressure to act *inclusively* and *equitably* toward the Somali community.[34]

This pattern of exploitation is not always measured in millions of dollars or dominated by shell organizations; it often involves rank-and-file newcomers taking advantage of public resources meant for others. A report in one of Canada's largest daily newspapers found that across the country, immigrants—particularly Indian international students—have been treating overburdened food banks as free grocery stores, calling them an "immigration perk."[35] Social media videos show them using the money saved on groceries to buy luxury items like video games and electronics. One student, who by law must be able to support himself to hold a visa, explained to his viewers in Hindi "how to get $500 in free food," while a couple encouraged others to "come taste Canada" while filming themselves in line at a foodbank with other Hindi-speaking newcomers.[36] The national news report also noted that newcomer use of food banks jumped from 13% to 34% of clients in just a few years, with minimal eligibility checks. It concluded that this abuse diverts donations from those in real need and erodes trust, making people less willing to give.

Immigration and Crime

And while the harm ethnic diversity does to social cohesion is clear, it's more difficult to determine the impact of increased diversity on crime, as the conclusions can be polar opposites depending on the researchers. On one side, a meta-analysis of 214 studies—mostly from the U.S.—found ethnic diversity was one of the strongest and most stable predictors of crime, with the greatest impact seen in violent crimes like homicide, assault, and robbery.[37] That work was corroborated by a 2011 study that examined data from 352 American cities that—over 30 years—experienced high levels of population growth, mostly due to immigration. It concluded that cities with high levels of ethnic heterogeneity (diversity) saw particularly high overall crime rates, especially when there was segregation due to co-ethnics forming enclaves.[38] Another similar study of 91 large U.S. cities conducted in 2019 determined that ethnic diversity is positively associated with higher violent and property crime rates. Moreover, highly diverse neighborhoods in less diverse cities had the highest levels of crime overall.[39]

But other studies argue that immigration—and the ethnic diversity it brings—doesn't increase crime and may even reduce it slightly. For example, an influential article published in 2018 in the *Annual Review of Criminology* reached that conclusion by combining a narrative review with a statistical meta-analysis.[40] In Canada, almost every government report and government-funded academic study also declares that immigration and the ethnic diversity it brings to communities lead to lower crime rates.[41]

For both the U.S. and Canada, the same reasons are given for the alleged lower rates. The studies note that immigrants are usually positively selected for pro-social characteristics—they come to work, build families, and purposely avoid trouble that could impact their ability to gain permanent residency.[42] Some immigrant communities—especially Chinese and other East Asian groups—also have strong family and social networks that discourage crime and promote stability.[43] However, it's those arguing that immigration *does not* increase crime in the U.S. and Canada who may have to reconsider their perspective. Their claim relies on data from periods when stricter vetting was in place and mostly or completely overlooks how permissive reforms from just the last decade, under the Biden and Trudeau administrations in the U.S. and Canada respectively, have prioritized higher immigration volumes over security, weakening previous safeguards.

We can concede that in the 1990s and early 2000s, the United States and Canada used more careful and thorough methods to evaluate and admit immigrants. In the U.S., the 1996 Illegal Immigration Reform and Immigrant Responsibility Act strengthened enforcement by introducing tougher penalties and measures to address illegal immigration, significantly boosting deportation rates from around 30,000 annually in 1990 to 400,000 by 2010.[44] During Donald Trump's first presidency (2017–2021), restrictions were increased through a ban on immigrants from 13 dangerous countries, reduced refugee admissions, and a "Remain in Mexico" policy for asylum seekers.[45]

In Canada, a points-based system prioritized economic immigrants with valuable skills and education to meet the needs of the labor market. The 2002 Immigration and Refugee Protection Act strengthened Canada's immigration process by selecting immigrants likely to contribute positively, requiring background checks, barring serious criminals, and streamlining deportation for those who failed screening.[46]

But in a very short time, all that changed radically.

Yesterday's Data vs. Today's Results

Under the Biden administration, many restrictive measures from the Trump era were reversed. Asylum seekers gained broader access, with America's southern border effectively left open to illegal migration. In 2023, various government-sanctioned humanitarian programs admitted hundreds of thousands of migrants from Cuba, Haiti, Nicaragua, and Venezuela with minimal vetting, while interior enforcement downplayed deportations for nonviolent offenders. Overall, removals of undocumented immigrants or offenders fell to half the levels seen under Trump.[47]

In Canada, Trudeau's Liberal government, elected in 2015, dramatically raised immigration targets from 300,000 in 2016 to about 500,000 by 2025, prioritizing diversity while relaxing rules. This amounted to roughly a 1% foreign-born population increase each year .[48] On top of these base immigration numbers, more than 1.5 million additional immigrants were admitted in 2023 alone under temporary work and study permits.[49] Entrants using these pathways faced almost no government scrutiny. In fact, investigations reveal that about 10% of individuals entering on "study permits" never set foot in the schools they were supposed to attend.[50] Moreover, another portion simply enrolled in fraudulent "institutions" run by co-ethnics that provided no actual instruction or classrooms.[51] The schools were merely a front used to expedite permanent residency; to a certain extent, the operators of the schools were "selling" Canadian citizenship.

In 2024, some caps were finally imposed amid glaring housing and public service strains,[52] but earlier lenient policies, along with expanded family reunification and loosely defined "refugee resettlement," had already gutted the system's protections. This occurred without the vetting resources needed to keep the process safe.

As further evidence of Canada's lax immigration standards, refugee claimants now effectively process themselves upon arrival, relying on an honor system. Border guards conduct minimal background checks and often accept self-reported information without challenge or follow-up. This near—open-door approach sacrifices national security for the sake of faster processing and political convenience.[53]

Returning our focus to crime specifically, when these pro-immigration studies were claiming immigration to be a neutral influence on lawlessness in the U.S. and Canada, the massive, less-vetted inflows under Biden and Trudeau had not yet worked their damage. We are now seeing emerging evidence that high immigration levels are contributing to elevated crime in both countries. Ten years ago, there were fewer stories of immigrants perpetrating acts of violence, theft, or significant motor vehicle violations ending in death; today such stories are a daily norm.

In light of conflicting reality, what should be made of the proliferation of pro-immigration studies? There may be a more sinister explanation. While I've been measured in explaining the disconnect between immigration narratives advanced by some sources—primarily on the political Left—and those offered elsewhere, others have been more blunt. For example, Alexander Kustov, an associate professor of migration in the Keough School of Global Affairs at the University of Notre Dame, attributes it to purposeful deception and academic malpractice.

Few scholars in North America have examined the politics and public opinion of immigration more closely than Kustov, and his conclusions are damning. As he puts it, "A lot of what liberal elites on both sides of the Atlantic say about immigration is deliberately misleading in ways that matter for policy and for democratic trust."[54]

Kustov's 2025 book,[55] and in particular his more recent writing,[56] deliver a factual and stinging critique of pro-immigration narratives. He argues that clear evidence of immigration's economic, fiscal, social, and security costs is routinely downplayed. He accuses officials and experts of misleading the public through selective framing, omissions, and half-truths. In particular, he notes that the humanitarian framing of immigration—which dominates the news and the speeches of progressive politicians—is misleading because it focuses on vulnerable cases while ignoring the fact that "most immigrants in the world are not humanitarian cases in the strict sense... less than 20% of all international migrants are refugees or asylum seekers, while the overwhelming majority move for work, family, or study."[57]

Although a liberal and self-described pro-immigration advocate himself, Kustov has been scorned and stigmatized by many of his ideological allies for exposing these uncomfortable truths. He admits,

Well-meaning colleagues have suggested that I soften or

> remove results that might 'feed the far right,' even when
> the estimates are robust. I have heard explicit advice
> not to emphasize negative fiscal impacts, violence spikes
> tied to specific policy failures, or integration problems
> in particular contexts—even when these are well docu
> mented.[58]

This impulse among the liberal elite to bury inconvenient facts has surfaced repeatedly in Canada. Internal memos to the Liberal government, obtained through access-to-information requests, show Immigration Department researchers advising senior officials to avoid public debate that might reveal actual immigration levels, noting that public support drops sharply once Canadians are informed of the true numbers.[59] The matter became explosive in 2025, when the Liberal government faced accusations of "purposeful censoring" after Immigration, Refugees and Citizenship Canada suspended its regular publication of monthly immigration datasets for several months following March. Although officials attributed the pause to a data redesign meant to provide better context, critics argued it was intended to obscure surging newcomer numbers—over 817,000 in the first four months of the year—to blunt public backlash amid mounting housing and infrastructure pressures.[60]

Crime Case Studies—U.S. and Canada

In the U.S., high-profile cases underscore the immigration-crime link. The 2024 murder of Laken Riley by Jose Ibarra, a Venezuelan migrant who entered illegally in 2022 and had previously been released after an arrest, sparked national outrage and exposed glaring vetting failures.[61] Other tragic incidents include the 2023 rape and murder of 12-year-old Jocelyn Nungaray in Houston by two Venezuelan migrants released at the border.[62] Numerous sexual assaults by migrants in New York City shelters have also been reported,[63] while rising gang activity in New York and Los Angeles has been linked to increasing migrant populations.[64] A 2023 report showed that increased illegal immigration under Biden brought a significant spike in crime, with two-thirds of all federal arrests involving noncitizens.[65]

Of course, not all the danger is rooted in sexual violence and gang activity. Illegal incidents involving immigrant truck drivers are becoming all too frequent. For example, in August 2025, Harjinder Singh, an undocumented truck driver who entered the U.S. illegally in 2018, caused a fatal crash on Florida's Turnpike. Singh had obtained commercial driver's licenses from California and Washington, states with virtually no enforcement of English proficiency requirements. Following the crash, federal assessments revealed that Singh failed English and road sign comprehension tests, answering only 2 of 12 English questions correctly and recognizing just 1 of 4 road signs.[66] Canada has seen a number of similar tragedies in which poorly trained men from India, hired by Canadian trucking companies—often Indian-owned—have caused fatal highway collisions. In one widely reported case, 31-year-old Sukhwinder Sidhu caused a multi-vehicle crash that killed former Canadian Olympic figure skater Alexandra Paul and injured her 10-month-old child while driving dangerously through a construction zone. Sidhu was traveling nearly double the reduced speed limit of 60 km/h, reaching close to the truck's top speed of approximately 108 km/h. He ignored warning signs and, in violation of safety regulations, had reportedly been driving for 26 hours.[67] The number of immigrants working in commercial trucking illegally is staggering. In just one of the 50 states, during a three-day crackdown in the fall of 2025, the Oklahoma Highway Patrol arrested 120 illegal immigrants, 91 of whom were illegally operating commercial trucks with licenses issued by progressives in a Democrat-run state; one of the licenses was issued without the driver providing a name.[68]

In Canada, Peel Region, just outside Toronto in the province of Ontario, stands as the country's most immigrant-dense area, with its two major cities, Mississauga and Brampton, ranking among the top municipalities for foreign-born residents. In both cities and the region as a whole, immigrants—most notably from India and the Middle East—make up more than half the population.[69]

Over the decade coinciding with the Liberal government's rollback of immigration safeguards—from 2015 to 2025—these areas have become notorious for exploding crime rates. To be sure, the mostly unregulated mass immigration of the last five years has pushed conditions from bad to catastrophic.

Car thefts in Peel Region exploded from 3,376 in 2020 to 7,231 in 2024—a staggering 114% increase. Property crimes such as shoplifting, fraud, and mischief also soared, climbing 63% from 23,325 incidents in 2020 to 37,972 in 2024. Carjackings surged 51% year-over-year from 2023 to 2024, nearly doubling, while violent home invasions skyrocketed by an alarming 306% over the same period.

Most strikingly, these violent home invasions—spreading from Peel Region into the Greater Toronto Area and most often linked to organized immigrant gangs[70]—have become so common that police now advise residents to make their vehicles easier to steal, in the hope that criminals will take the car and spare the family. As one warning from police put it: "To prevent the possibility of being attacked in your home, leave your [key] fobs at your front door."[71] Surrey, British Columbia, competes with Peel Region and its cities of Mississauga and Brampton for the title of having the highest proportions of immigrants relative to native-born residents. In Surrey, data from 2021 reported that nearly half of residents were not born in Canada.[72] Despite being on the opposite side of Canada from Peel Region, the same pattern appears: higher levels of immigration correlate with higher levels of crime.

Of particular note, in late 2025 and early 2026, Surrey police linked a record-breaking surge in extortion to newly organized crime networks run by Indian (Punjabi) nationals. Businesses and individuals were threatened—often through social media—and told to pay cryptocurrency. When they refused, shootings and arson targeting homes and businesses were common. Of the few suspects arrested, many were found to have entered Canada on student visas or work permits and remained after their status expired, with little or no enforcement monitoring those overstays.[73]

In these various cases, despite photos showing the ethnicity of the perpetrators, records reflecting Indian or Middle Eastern names, and, in some cases, citizenship documentation confirming illegal or temporary status, mainstream media and police reports often obscure their non-citizen standing. Instead, they rely on vague descriptions such as "men from the Peel Region" or "suspects living in Surrey."[74]

Crime and Immigration—The Lesson of Europe

While progressive elites in both the U.S. and Canada do their best to obscure the links between immigration and rising crime, outside of North America, in the Western nations of Europe, the association is so glaring it simply cannot be hidden. There, in country after country, the statistics show that immigrants—particularly non-Western, foreign-born individuals—commit crimes at rates far higher than their share of the population.

In Denmark, non-Western immigrants make up 8–10% of the population but account for 25–30% of violent crime suspects, a three- to fourfold over-representation.[75] In Finland, foreign-born individuals are 8% of the population yet represent 20% of crime suspects, with a threefold overrepresentation in violent crimes.[76] In Sweden, foreign-born persons comprise 20% of the population but 33% of all crime suspects, with up to a fivefold overrepresentation in violent and sexual offenses.[77] Norway sees non-Western immigrants at 10% of the population, accounting for 25% of crime suspects, roughly 2.5 times their share.[78]

In Germany, non-German nationals are 13% of the population but 30% of crime suspects, while asylum seekers, just 3% of the population, make up 12% of those arrested for violent crime.[79] In France, foreign nationals represent about 7% of the population yet account for 24% of arrests, a threefold overrepresentation.[80] In the UK, non-UK nationals are 10% of the population but represent 20% of crime suspects and 21% of prisoners, with a 2.5 times overrepresentation in sexual offenses.[81] Especially significant is that, in the UK, Muslim immigrants are becoming known for their terrorist tendencies. Though they comprise only about 6.5% of the overall population of Britain,[82] they are convicted of about 65% of domestic terrorism offenses.[83]

Progressive politicians suggest that diversity is a strength measurable in cultural enrichment and social dynamism. More factually, the best research and statistics suggest it's better measured in social fragmentation and arrest rates. As we will see next, it is also linked to economic decline.

The Economics of Immigration

You cannot have mass migration and a welfare state; the two are mutually exclusive. When vast numbers of newcomers, who have previously contributed nothing to the system, immediately gain access to public benefits—education, healthcare, job training, social assistance, food banks—those programs inevitably strain, decline, and eventually collapse. Too little is paid in; too much is taken out.

Before U.S. President Roosevelt's New Deal in the 1930s and the birth of the welfare state, immigrants to America came with no expectation of public support—only the chance to succeed through hard work. Back then, without taxpayer-funded safety nets to soften failure, many simply went home when success did not materialize. In fact, more than half of the southern and eastern Europeans who arrived in America in the early 1900s eventually returned to their countries of origin.[84] Today, almost no one leaves once they get in. Newcomers know that living in government-subsidized "poverty" in America is still more affluent and secure than a working man's lot in parts of India or Africa. In Canada, the failure to find gainful employment is even less of a disincentive to leave. All health care—not merely access for the poorest residents—is fully funded by working taxpayers, and immigrants are immediately eligible. Canadian citizens spend $1 billion per year to provide full health coverage to refugee claimants alone, and according to a Parliamentary Budget Officer report, "between now and 2030, Canadians are on track to spend $6.2 billion on health care for refugees or refugee claimants"—none of whom have contributed to the system. What they receive is "a higher level of care than that enjoyed by the average Canadian citizen. In addition to hospital care and surgical care... [they also receive] dental care, vision care, pharmacare and other services not typically covered by public health plans." Even when refugee status is denied (because the claim was fraudulent), the government has no effective means of preventing them from continuing to receive full health benefits.[85]

Outside of health benefits, refugee claimants certainly, and immigrants generally, also receive government financial supports the likes of which do not exist for the country's most destitute native citizens.[86] To be sure, an immigrant and his family can do very well living on government assistance alone. For example, the Canada Child Benefit (CCB) is a tax-free monthly payment for families with children under 18. Like other welfare programs, newcomers disproportionately benefit due to their lower incomes and larger families, and they have the same eligibility as citizens. The poorest applicants—many immigrants fall into this category—receive $7,997 per child under 6 and $6,748 for children 6 to 17 in 2025–26. So, an immigrant family with four children under six gets $32,000 per year; four children over six earns about $27,000.[87] The unemployed or low-income immigrant is also eligible for almost free daycare (about $10 per day) so, in theory, they can have their children cared for by taxpayers.[88] The internet and social media are filled with "influencers" of Indian origin living in Canada who actively encourage migration by telling their audiences that the Canadian government will pay for their children.[89]

As the financial figures above hint, the claim that immigration is a net benefit to the economy is false. While many immigrants are industrious from the moment they are eligible to work in the U.S. and Canada, research demonstrates that, beginning in the 1990s, when immigration rates began to rise, the economic benefits from immigration began to fall.

In America, the evidence that immigration was doing harm to native-born citizens in general was confirmed beyond doubt in 1997 in the National Research Council study *The New Americans*.[90] The researchers—drawn from the top economists at America's most elite universities—determined that, in raw numbers, immigration contributed a trivial one-tenth of one percent to GDP, but that was before the costs of welfare, education, health care, and other social programs provided to immigrants were factored in.

Once the true full cost immigrants impose on the public purse was calculated, the researchers concluded that native-born households in the U.S. paid about $200 a year more in taxes because of immigration.[91] Moreover, the cost to native-born citizens ballooned to over $1000 per family in states like California, where immigration was highest.[92] One of the leaders of the study, Harvard economist George Borjas, summarized the findings, stating, "Whatever the 'immigration surplus,' it's eaten away by the cost of providing services to immigrants."[93]

Following his work on the *The New Americans* study, Borjas spent the next two decades examining the effects of immigration on the economy. He summarized his peer-reviewed findings in his 2013 report "Immigration and the American Worker" and his 2014 book *Immigration Economics*.[94] He noted that increases in immigration numbers—especially for low-skilled immigrants soon joined by family members—imposed a lifetime net cost of $80,000 to $100,000 per native American.[95] Working-class Americans in low-wage jobs were hardest hit; they were doubly affected by immigration.

Simply put, because the number of available positions in the job market is limited, when immigrants enter the workforce, more people compete for the same jobs, giving employers greater leverage in setting wages. With a larger pool of applicants, employers know they can offer lower pay without risking unfilled positions, since many workers are willing to accept the job. Many immigrants, accustomed to subsistence conditions in their home countries, are willing to work for wages that are only modestly higher than what they earned before—levels that native workers may consider barely livable.

This dynamic places downward pressure on wages for low-skilled native workers. Accordingly, Borjas found that from the 1960s through the 2010s, every 10% increase in immigration was associated with about a 4% decline in the wages of the poorest native Americans, making escape from poverty nearly impossible.[96]

Traditional conservatives view the use of foreign workers as a means of wage suppression as a betrayal of their most vulnerable countrymen, and they direct their anger toward globalist corporations that value ever-expanding profit margins over national loyalty. To mask their greed, the corporate defense often claims that native citizens are reluctant to fill certain positions. Ironically, even when this is true, it's often a problem of their own making: years of stagnant wages have rendered these jobs unattractive to citizens seeking a standard of living comparable to that of their parents.

Current political leaders on both the Left and the Right perpetuate this system, advancing immigration policies that serve corporate funders while simultaneously expanding their electoral base among the very newcomers whose arrival has displaced native constituents.

Working with a researcher from Statistics Canada, a Canadian government agency, Borjas conducted a similar analysis on immigration's impact on wages north of the U.S. border. The results were identical, with a 10% increase in immigration leading to about a 4% decrease in the wages of native Canadians.[97] Similarly, research by Canadian economists shows that, even decades after arriving, immigrants in Canada tend to use more public resources than they contribute to the economy. One 2015 study tracking immigrants from the 1980s into 2010 found that, on average, they received $18,000 in government benefits from all levels of government but contributed only $13,000 in taxes, meaning that, as a group, immigrants typically drew about $5,000 more from the public purse than they put in.[98]

The Groups Vying for "Greatest Drain on the Public Purse"

Research shows that the strain immigrants place on the welfare system is exacerbated by newcomers hailing from certain parts of the world. Evidence from many European countries indicates that immigrants from the Middle East, North Africa, Pakistan, and Turkey (collectively referred to as MENAPT countries) are far less likely to contribute economically and far more likely to rely on state welfare programs, even decades after arrival.

In Denmark, a Ministry of Finance report (2018) analyzing data from 2014 to 2018 found that immigrants from MENAPT countries impose an annual net fiscal cost of billions, reflecting both higher usage of welfare benefits and lower tax contributions. Among non-Western immigrants, 50–60% still receive social assistance more than ten years after arrival, and 30–40% remain dependent long after 15 years.[99]

Similar patterns emerge across Europe. A 2017 European Commission study focusing on refugees—many from the Middle East—found that 10 to 15 years after arrival, employment rates for these individuals remain low, with half not working. These patterns often persist into the second generation.[100] The United Kingdom shows comparable trends. According to a 2022 Migration Observatory briefing, Middle Eastern refugees experience persistent economic inactivity. Overall, 40–50% of this group relies on long-term welfare benefits, compared with 15–20% for native residents.[101] A House of Commons Library report from 2025 further confirms that asylum seekers from the Middle East—primarily Pakistan, Afghanistan, Iran, and Syria—show slow economic independence, with 35% remaining on welfare after ten years or more, two to three times higher than for UK-born residents.[102]

In addition to being a net drain on public resources and a key factor in wage suppression, the economic ripple effects of immigration can be seen in housing prices and hospital access being pushed out of reach of native citizens. Conservative estimates show that an average immigration rate of 1% is associated with a real home price increase of 3% per year.[103] In areas where immigrants congregate heavily, increases can be many times higher than that figure.[104] Because most Americans rely on private healthcare, in the U.S. the strain of mass immigration on hospitals and clinics is felt most acutely by the poorest citizens, who must compete with newcomers for limited public health resources. In contrast, Canada's universal healthcare system spreads the impact of mass immigration across the entire population, with native Canadians increasingly facing longer wait times and reduced access to medical care as the system struggles to accommodate too many immigrants and too few doctors and nurses.[105] Beyond the pressure of sheer numbers, some reports indicate that immigrants tend to make heavier use of healthcare services—especially hospital emergency rooms—further intensifying the burden on the system.[106]

Looking Inward

This chapter began by observing that Traditional Conservatism upholds nationalism: the principle that a nation's citizens must take priority over the interests of outsiders and that government leaders must design their country's policies to serve the well-being of their own people. Currently, the elected officials of America—and especially those in Canada—often do not put the well-being of their own people first.

Though immigration must be addressed (and I say how in the next section), the first corrective step is to look inward rather than outward. To rebuild unity through a cohesive national culture, both the U.S. and Canada must make a deliberate shift. Specifically, the state should heartily acknowledge and celebrate the European settlers who built North American civilization from the ground up. Just as importantly, it must also recognize and support the Christian norms and values that shaped that exceptional success. This acclaim must be public and persuasive. Support for multiculturalism must be abandoned, and unity through shared heritage must become the norm. There will be tolerance of difference, but cultural relativism with its claim that "all cultures are equal" will be categorically rejected.

Conversely, ideologies that explicitly promote the denigration and overthrow of this civilization birthed by these European founders and their Christianity-inspired principles should be made illegal. Supporters of proven anti-Western ideologies should be jailed or, where applicable, deported. I'll develop this argument further in Chapter 9, but it rests on the fact that a nation cannot *defend* itself unless it can *define* itself.[107]

In this axiom, to "defend" a nation means not only to protect its borders or military interests but also to sustain its way of life—to protect everything that makes it *distinctly itself.* However, a nation cannot protect what it does not clearly understand. To "define" itself means having a firm grasp of who it is, where it came from, and what it stands for: its historical roots, founding principles, and core cultural values. Without this definition, there is no common standard by which to recognize threats or determine what is worth preserving.

When a nation loses sight of its defining identity, it becomes vulnerable in several ways. Cultural erosion sets in first: without shared values or a coherent national story, the population becomes fragmented and easily swayed by outside influences that dilute or replace the native culture. This is often followed by political confusion, as leaders who no longer understand or affirm their nation's purpose craft policies serving transient interests rather than a coherent national good. Finally, there is moral disarmament. A people unsure of their moral foundations lack the confidence to assert their interests, defend their traditions, or resist ideologies that contradict their heritage.

By contrast, nations that understand their historical origins and core convictions are better equipped to sustain themselves. They know what they are protecting and why it matters. In this sense, definition precedes defense: only a people who know who they are can recognize what threatens them, what deserves their loyalty, and what must be preserved for future generations.

Looking Outward

America and Canada risk becoming mere places on a map rather than distinct nations with defining traits if almost everything about the current immigration systems does not change. Both the quantity and quality of immigrants must be addressed.

In terms of numbers, a complete moratorium on the entrance of newcomers is likely warranted for the next decade or two, followed by stringent, highly selective limitations thereafter. Pausing inflows allows time for assimilation, giving immigrants the time and space to disperse geographically and adopt local norms. Without this pause, enclaves persist, parallel societies develop, and, among the native population, hostility toward foreigners grows, leading to greater fracturing of social cohesion. Halting immigration would also ease the burden on current public institutions, which have been overwhelmed by the volume of new arrivals. If allowed to catch up, efficiency could be restored, and a focus on serving citizens could once again become the primary mission of these institutions.

Critics, often globalist elites or business lobbyists, decry such measures as economically suicidal, warning of labor shortages and stunted growth. Yet, their perspective overlooks the adaptive capacity of an independent, self-reliant economy. Yes, adaptation will entail short-term disruptions: some industries may face higher costs, leading to modestly elevated prices for goods and services. But this trade-off brings major benefits, including more opportunities for native workers as labor markets tighten, pushing businesses to invest in training and automation instead of relying on cheap foreign labor.

Because wages will increase, citizens will be pleased to fill roles in construction, agriculture, tech, and other fields that previously saw their wages depressed by imported competition. Other economic benefits will follow. Housing markets, strained by current population growth, would stabilize, lowering prices and making homeownership more accessible to native-born families.

Hungary offers a clear example of a nation significantly limiting immigration inflows without courting economic disaster. Despite limiting immigration to about 1 per 1,000 people—compared with about 10 in the UK and 4 in France—Hungary performs better than these countries on key economic indicators, showing the success of its pro-citizen approach. Its 2024 unemployment rate of 4.1% is lower than France's 7.4% and slightly better than the UK's 4.4%, reflecting a labor market that prioritizes native workers.

Public debt is about 74.5% of GDP, well below the UK's 100.5% and France's 110.6%, signaling stronger fiscal discipline. Prices are about 35% below the EU average, attracting $120 billion in manufacturing investment. While GDP growth (0.5% in 2024) trails the UK and France (both 1.1%), Hungary's focus on social cohesion, low debt, and tight labor markets shows that restrictive immigration does not harm economic stability or overall competitiveness.[108]

Moreover, the globalists, corporate lobbyists, and pandering politicians who have made mass immigration their central policy tool—and sell it as the primary solution to labor shortages—rarely factor the rapid advance of artificial intelligence (AI) into their economic equations, a profound strategic mistake. AI is reshaping the global job market, and even major progressive institutions such as the World Economic Forum warn that it will soon eliminate tens of millions of low-skill jobs, even as it creates a handful of new ones for which most immigrants are far less likely to be qualified.[109]

This cannot be stressed enough: the jobs most vulnerable to AI automation are precisely those in which newcomers are concentrated: warehouse picking, farm labor, basic manufacturing, and service work, resulting in an expanding surplus of workers for roles that are disappearing.

Layered onto this is the aggressive push into humanoid robotics by entrepreneurs like Tesla CEO Elon Musk. For example, Musk's Optimus robots aim to make human physical labor optional. By late 2026, the Optimus Gen 3 prototype will be nearing commercial readiness, equipped with highly dexterous hands, advanced vision systems, and an efficient AI chip capable of everything from folding laundry to handling factory materials. Tesla plans to deploy thousands of units in its own factories and ramp up to mass production in the following years. Ultimately, it aims to produce hundreds of thousands—and eventually millions—of units annually at a price point below $20,000.[110]

In short, many new arrivals are being funneled into roles on the verge of disappearing. If even a fraction of this vision materializes, the manual labor positions that currently justify large inflows of immigrant workers will soon be performed by machines. As these jobs vanish, welfare rolls will rise, deficits will grow, and social tensions will deepen, especially in communities already struggling with unemployment and strained public resources.

Regarding the "quality" of incoming immigrants, unless the U.S. and Canada return to prioritizing those whose beliefs, customs, and values align with their own, their countries' historical beliefs, customs, and values will gradually disappear. As cultural commentator and pastor Doug Wilson has observed, if you continue to replace the sugar in a sugar bowl with white sand, at some point it's no longer a bowl of sugar. Just as sugar differs significantly from sand, research shows that the Christian beliefs, customs, and values underpinning the U.S. and Canada differ—in superior ways—from others and have the unique ability to bring individual and social flourishing. Thus, the brutal reality is that drawing immigrants from non-Christian nations comparatively brings what most in the West would consider inferior mores and eventually less societal success.

Should there be a religious test placed on immigrants in which their commitment to Christ is a necessary criterion for consideration as a citizen? In keeping with the tenets of Traditional Conservatism, the answer is no. Certainly many native-born Americans and Canadians could not pass such a test and would rightly condemn any politician trying to impose it as a tyrannical theocrat. Traditional conservatives do not want to be in the company of countries like Saudi Arabia, where the path to citizenship is unavailable without conversion.[111] But there are ways outside of directly policing religious convictions to increase the odds that future immigrants endorse quintessential Western culture with its Christian norms and values.

For example, directly policing criteria of cultural alignment is fair game. At minimum, a demonstrated ability in spoken and written English before arrival should be non-negotiable.[112] Passing a cultural compatibility test should be as well.

Unlike current "values-based" tests used by some Western countries, a newly conceived exam would more rigorously interrogate the beliefs and practices of prospective newcomers for their sincere dedication to "Western-ness." It would be conducted by trained interviewers who would be assisted by AI facial monitoring software in determining untruthful and deceptive responses. As reported recently in the top science journal *Nature*, such AI technology already exists and can detect lies with over 80% accuracy, and it's improving by the day.[113]

Thorough background checks in the applicant's native country would also be conducted. To the skeptics insisting that there would not be the time or resources for such stringent measures, they should recall that under a Traditional Conservative government immigration numbers will be reduced to a minuscule fraction, and state funding for newcomers—typical under progressive regimes—would be eliminated altogether, freeing up money for this necessary vetting.

Of course, one of the key means of ensuring cultural continuity from immigrants is to employ source country weighting. Applicants from Western nations with Christian roots would be prioritized. The same preference would apply to those from non-Western communities known for being Christian or for living fairly and peacefully with Christians while upholding historically Western norms and values. Conversely, intake would be significantly reduced or terminated completely from regions with low institutional trust, religious persecution of Christians, or values in conflict with Western norms.

Finally, as discussed in Chapter 1, citizenship under a Traditional Conservative government would come much more slowly, allowing for the true characteristics of the newcomers to manifest. If, over the course of a decade or so, immigrants are without evidence of cultural assimilation and consistent contribution to the economy and community, they would be deported.

In light of these propositions, traditional conservatives might be accused of animosity toward foreigners. That is a mischaracterization. To paraphrase G.K. Chesterton: The traditional conservative limits immigrants not because he hates *them*, but because he loves his countrymen.

Endnotes for Chapter 3

1. Robert D. Putnam, "E Pluribus Unum: Diversity and Community in the Twenty-First Century," *Scandinavian Political Studies* 30, no. 2 (2007): 137–174, https://doi.org/10.1111/j.1467-9477.2007.00176.x.

2. Michael Jonas, "The Downside of Diversity: A Harvard Political Scientist Finds That Diversity Hurts Civic Life," *Boston Globe*, August 5, 2007, https://people.uncw.edu/imperialm/UNCW/PLS_502/B_Globe_Diversity_ Putnam_8_5_07.pdf.

3. Ibid.

4. See Putman, "E Pluribus Unum."

5. Ilana Mercer, quoted in Jonas, "The Downside of Diversity."

6. Jonas, "The Downside of Diversity." See also: Putman, "E Pluribus Unum."

7. Ibid.

8. Tom van der Meer and Jochem Tolsma, "Ethnic Diversity and Its Effects on Social Cohesion," *Annual Review of Soci-*

ology 40 (2014): 459–78, https://doi. org/10.1146/annurev
-soc-071913-043309.

9. Putnam, "E Pluribus Unum," 149.

10. van der Meer and Tolsma, "Ethnic Diversity and Its Effects,"
15.

11. Ibid.

12. In the paper "Ethnic Diversity and Its Effects on Social Cohesion" to explain why the U.S. suffers most under ethnic
diversity the authors provide socially progressive answers that
unfairly demonize Americans. I've taken their findings about
multiculturalism and expressed it in a way that I believe is
more accurate and fair to the American people.

13. See: Ruud Koopmans and Stine Veit, "Trust Is in the Eye
of the Beholder: How Perceptions of Local Diversity and
Segregation Shape Social Cohesion," *Social Forces* 93, no.
1 (2014): 141–67; James Laurence, "Does Ethnic Diversity
Have a Negative Effect on Attitudes towards the Commu-
nity? A Longitudinal Analysis of the Causal Claims within
the Ethnic Diversity and Social Cohesion Debate," *European
Sociological Review* 31, no. 5 (2015): 613–27; James Lau-
rence and Lee Bentley, "Diversity or Disadvantage? Putnam,
Goodhart, Ethnic Heterogeneity, and Collective Efficacy-
" *Environment and Planning A* 48, no. 4 (2016): 663–84;
James Laurence, "Ethnic Diversity, Ethnic Threat, and Social
Cohesion: (Re)-Evaluating the Role of Perceived Out-Group
Threat and Prejudice in the Diversity/ Cohesion Relation-

ship," *Social Science Research* 64 (2017): 155–68.

14. Peter Thisted Dinesen, Merlin Schaeffer, and Kim Mannemar Sønderskov, "Ethnic Diversity and Social Trust: A Narrative and Meta-Analytical Review," *Annual Review of Political Science* 23 (2020): 441–465, https://doi. org/10.1 146/annurev-polisci-052918-020708.

15. Ibid.

16. Ibid.

17. David Hugh-Jones, "Honesty, Beliefs About Honesty, and Economic Growth in 15 Countries," *Journal of Economic Behavior & Organization* 127 (July 2016): 99–114, https://doi.org/10.1016/j.jebo.2016.04.012; See also: David Hugh-Jones, "Honesty and Beliefs About Honesty in 15 Countries," University of East Anglia School of Economics Working Paper Series 2015-01 (September 2015), https://ueaeco.github.io/working-papers/papers/ ueaeco/UEA -ECO-15-01.pdf.

18. Ibid.

19. Alain Cohn, Michel André Maréchal, David Tannenbaum, and Christian Lukas Zünd, "Civic Honesty Around the Globe," *Science* 365, no. 6458 (July 19, 2019): 70–73, https://doi.org/10.1126/science.aau8712.

20. Ibid.

21. Yann Algan and Pierre Cahuc, "Inherited Trust and

Growth," *American Economic Review* 100, no. 5 (2010): 2060–92, https://doi.org/10.1257/ aer.100.5.2060.

22. Ibid.

23. Ibid.

24. For example: Larry Pynn, "I just received freedom-of-information documents from UBC related to student cheating by nationality over three years," August 16, 2019, https:/ /x.com/lpynn/status/1162413231207415808; Charles Rusnell, "40 University of Alberta Computing Science Students Caught Cheating," March 4, 2020, *CBC News*, https://ww w.cbc.ca/news/canada/ edmonton/u-of-a-computing-cheating-1.5483278; Sophie Hogan, "Nearly half of US Chinese student dismissals due to 'academic dishonesty'," May 21, 2024, *The Pie News*, https://thepienews.com/academic-dishonesty-common-reason-dismissal-chinese-intl-students/.

25. Shounak Sanyal, "Fake Degree Racket in Kerala Sets Off Political Firestorm in Australia," *India Today*, January 7, 2026, https://www.indiatoday.in/world/story/fake-degree-scam-racket-across-india-sets-off-political-firestorm-in-australia-malcolm-roberts-antony-albanese-indians-2848095-2026-01-07.

26. Federal Bureau of Investigation, "Internet Crime Complaint Center 2023 Annual Report," https://www.ic3.gov/Media/PDF/AnnualReport/2023_IC3Report.pdf.

27. U.S. Department of Justice, "Five Chinese Nationals Indicted in $27 Million Elder Fraud Scheme," March 15, 2024, https://www.justice.gov/usao-sdca/pr/five-chinese-nationals-indicted-scamming-seniors-out-more-27-million.

28. U.S. Department of Justice, "Indian Nationals Convicted of Money Laundering Conspiracy That Took Life Savings from Victims in Ohio, Michigan, Illinois, and Indiana," February 4, 2025, https://www.justice.gov/ usao-ndoh/pr/indian-nationals-convicted-money-laundering-conspiracy-took-life-savings-victims-ohio.

29. Seth Kaplan, "Fraud in Minnesota: Detailing the Nearly $1 Billion in Schemes," *FOX 9 Minneapolis-St. Paul*, December 8, 2025, https://www. fox9.com/news/fraud-minnesota-detailing-nearly-1-billion-schemes; Joe Walsh, "What to Know about Minnesota Fraud Allegations, as Trump Levels Attacks on Walz," *CBS News*, December 4, 2025, https://www.cbsnews.com/ news/what-to-know-about-minnesota-fraud-allegations-as-trump-levels-attacks-on-walz/.

30. Ibid.

31. Rich McHugh and Anna Kutz, "What Is the Minnesota Social Aid Fraud Scandal About?," *NewsNation*, December 29, 2025, https://www.newsnationnow.com/crime/minnesota-aid-fraud-scheme-somali-timeline-explainer; Jonah Kaplan and Joe Walsh, "Everything We Know about Minnesota's Massive Fraud Schemes," *CBS News*, January 5, 2026, https:// www.cbsnews.com/news/minnesota-fraud-s

chemes-what-we-know.

32. Nick Schifrin, "Federal Agents Probe Fraud Allegations Targeting Somali Child Care Providers in Minnesota," *PBS NewsHour*, December 30, 2025, https://www.pbs.org/newshour/show/federal-agents-probe-fraud-allegations-targeting-somali-child-care-providers-in-minnesota.

33. Jonah Kaplan, "Luxury Cars and Private Villas: See How Minnesota Fraudsters Spent Millions Intended for Hungry Kids," *CBS News*, December 11, 2025, https://www.cbsnews.com/news/minnesota-fraud-spent-millions-luxury-cars-villas/.

34. Jonah Kaplan, "Minnesota Officials Saw Signs of Massive Fraud Even before COVID Hit," December 8, 2025, *CBS News*, https://www.cbsnews.com/news/minnesota-fraud-signs-before-covid/; Max Rego, "Omar: There Were 'Always Those Alarms' about COVID-Era Minnesota Fraud Scheme," *The Hill*, December 7, 2025, https://thehill.com/homenews/house/5638029-somali-community-impact-fraud/.

35. Jamie Sarkonak, "When Your Food-Bank Donations Subsidize Fraud and Video Games," *National Post*, March 18, 2025, https://nationalpost.com/ opinion/jamie-sarkonak-when-your-food-bank-donations-subsidize-fraud-and-video-games.

36. Ibid.

37. Travis C. Pratt and Francis T. Cullen, "Assessing Macro-Level Predictors and Theories of Crime: A Meta-Analysis," *Crime and Justice* 32 (2005): 373–450.

38. John R. Hipp, "Spreading the Wealth: The Effect of the Distribution of Income and Race/Ethnicity across Households and Neighborhoods on City Crime Trajectories," *Criminology* 49, no. 3 (2011): 631–665.

39. Marin R. Wenger, "Clarifying the Relationship Between Racial Diversity and Crime: Neighborhoods Versus Cities," *Crime & Delinquency* 65, no. 11 (2019): 1513–36.

40. Graham C. Ousey and Charis E. Kubrin, "Immigration and Crime: Assessing a Contentious Issue," *Annual Review of Criminology* 1 (2018): 63–84, https://prohic.nl/wp-content/uploads/2020/11/8 2-27juli2020-ImmigrationCrimeMeta.pdf.

41. For example: Maria Jung, "Immigration and Crime in Canadian Cities: A 35-Year Study," *Canadian Journal of Criminology and Criminal Justice* 62, no. 1 (2020): 71–97, doi:10.3138/cjccj.2019-0015; Haimin Zhang, *Impact of Immigration on Canada: Crime, Wage, and Diversity* (Ph.D. diss., University of British Columbia, 2014); Martin A. Andresen, "International Immigration, Internal Migration, and Homicide in Canadian Provinces," *International Journal of Offender Therapy and Comparative Criminology* 57, no. 5 (May 2013): 632–657, doi:10.1177/0306624X12436798; Ronit Dinovitzer, John Hagan, and Ron Levi, "Immigration and Youthful Illegalities in a Global Edge City," *Social Forces*

88, no. 1 (2009): 337–372, doi:10.1353/sof.0.0229; Statistics Canada, "Immigrants at less risk of violent crime" (analysis article / Juristat material summarizing survey results and trends; updated summaries and related StatCan publications on immigrant victimization and crime trends).

42. Ibid. Also see Ousey and Kubrin, "Immigration and Crime."

43. Shamim Ara Pia, "Comparing Asian Immigrants Offending Rates with Other Immigrants" (Master's thesis, Illinois State University, 2024), https:// ir.library.illinoisstate.edu/cgi/viewcontent.cgi?article=2939&context=etd.

44. Donald Kerwin, "From IIRIRA to Trump: Connecting the Dots to the Current US Immigration Policy Crisis," *Journal on Migration and Human Security* 6, no. 3 (2018): 7–10, https://doi. org/10.1177/2331502418786718; U.S. Department of Homeland Security, Office of Homeland Security Statistics, *2019 Yearbook of Immigration Statistics* (Washington, DC: DHS, 2020), table 39, https://ohss.dhs.gov/ topics/immigration/yearbook/2019/table39; Jacqueline Maria Hagan, Nestor Rodriguez, and Brianna Castro, "Deporting Social Capital: Implications for Immigrant Communities in the United States," *Journal of Ethnic and Migration Studies* 46, no. 13 (2020): 2661–66, https://doi.org/10.1080/136 9183X.2018.1510378.

45. Kristina Cooke and Mica Rosenberg, American Immigration Council, "Trump Plans to Slash U.S . Refugee Admissions to New Low," *Reuters*, October 1, 2020, https://www.reuters.com/world/us/trump-plans-sl

ash-us-refugee-admissions-new-low-2020-10-01/; "Migrant Protection Protocols," fact sheet, February 1, 2024, American Immigration Council, https://www. americanimmigra tioncouncil.org/fact-sheet/migrant-protection-protocols/.

46. A.E. Challinor, "Canada's Immigration Policy: A Focus on Human Capital," September 15, 2011, Migration Policy Institute, https://www. migrationpolicy.org/article/ca nadas-immigration-policy-focus-human-capital; Tariq Ahmad, "Canada: Points-Based Immigration System," Library of Congress, March 4, 2013, https://tile.loc.gov/storage-ser vices/service/ll/ llglrd/2019670576/2019670576.pdf.

47. Muzaffar Chishti, Kathleen Bush-Joseph, Colleen Putzel-Kavanaugh, and Madeleine Greene, "Biden's Mixed Immigration Legacy: Border Challenges Overshadowed Modernization Advances," Migration Policy Institute, December 10, 2024, https://www.migrationpolicy.org/articl e/ biden-immigration-legacy; Jens Manuel Krogstad and Ana Gonzalez-Barrera, "Key facts about U.S. immigration policies and Biden's proposed changes," January 11 , 2022, *Pew Research Center*, https://www.pewresear ch. org/short-reads/2022/01/11/key-facts-about-u-s-immi gration-policies-and-bidens-proposed-changes/; Kristen E. Eichensehr, "Immigration and Migration: Biden Administration Reverses Trump Administration Policies on Immigration and Asylum," *American Journal of International Law* 115, no. 2 (2021): 340–47, https://doi.org/10.1017/aj il.2021.15.

48. Government of Canada, "An Immigration Plan to Grow the Economy," November 1, 2022, https://www.canada.ca/en/immigration-refugees-citizenship/news/2022/11/an-immigration-plan-to-grow-the-economy.html; Promit Mukherjee, "Canada Clocks Fastest Population Growth in 66 Years in 2023," *Reuters*, March 27, 2024, https://www.reuters.com/world/americas/canada-clocks-fastest-population-growth-66-years-2023-2024-03-27/.

49. Government of Canada, Immigration, Refugees and Citizenship Canada, 2024, "Question Period Note: Temporary Worker Program," Reference number IRCC-2024-QP-00068, November 19, 2024 (Ottawa: Government of Canada, 2024), https://search.open.canada.ca/qpnotes/record/cic,IRCC-2024-QP-00068.

50. Marie Woolf, "Nearly 50,000 Foreign Students Listed as 'No-Shows' by Canadian Schools," *The Globe and Mail*, January 15, 2025, https://www.theglobeandmail.com/politics/article-international-students-school-attendance-data/; Marie Woolf, "More than 10,000 Foreign Student Acceptance Letters May Be Fake, Says Top Immigration Official," *The Globe and Mail*, November 15, 2024, https://www.t heglobeandmail.com/politics/ article-more-than-10000-foreign-student-acceptance-letters-may-be-fake-says/.

51. Karan Yadav, "20,000 Indian Students Vanish in Canada: Visa Scams, Fake Colleges, and a Broken System," *The Times*

of India, February 8, 2025, https://timesofindia.indiatimes.com/education/news/20000-indian-students-vanish-in-canada-visa-scams-fake-colleges-and-a-broken-system/ articleshow/118026610.cms.

52. "Canada to Set Targets to Decrease the Number of New Temporary Residents for the First Time," *Associated Press*, March 21, 2024, https://apnews.com/ article/6f78ae6e3a3d0fe92f23be62533b2868.

53. Terence Corcoran, "FIRST READING: Migrants Are Being Screened on the Honour System, MPs Told," *National Post*, November 21, 2025, https:// nationalpost.com/opinion/migrants-screened-honour-system-mps-told.

54. Alexander Kustov, "The Uncomfortable Truths About Immigration," *Popular by Design* (Substack newsletter), January 22, 2026, https://alexanderkustov. substack.com/p/the-uncomfortable-truths-about-immigration.

55. Alexander Kustov, *In Our Interest: How Democracies Can Make Immigration Popular* (New York: Columbia University Press, 2025).

56. Kustov, "The Uncomfortable Truths About Immigration."

57. Ibid.

58. Ibid.

59. Teresa Wright, "Feds Warned of Tipping Point in Public Support for Immigration Levels,"

CTV News, April 13, 2018, https://www.ctvnew s. ca/politics/article/feds-warned-of-tipping-point-in-pub-lic-support-for-immigration-levels/.

60. Michelle Rempel Garner, "Canadians Have a Right to Know Our Immigration Numbers," Conservative Party of Canada, August 11, 2025, https://www.conservative.ca/canad ians-have-a-right-to-know-our-immigration-numbers/; Brian Lilley, "LILLEY: Carney's Liberals Hiding Immigration Data as Questions Mount," *Toronto Sun*, August 11, 2025, https://torontosun.com/opinion/columnists/carney s-liberals-hiding-immigration-data-as-questions-mount.

61. Nadine Yousif, "US Nursing Student Laken Riley's Killer Sentenced to Life," *BBC News*, November 20, 2024, https ://www.bbc.com/news/articles/ c23829939rjo20.

62. Rosa Flores, Dakin Andone, and Sara Weisfeldt, "Jocelyn Nungaray: Houston 12-Year-Old's Killing Becomes Focus of Immigration Debate as 2 Undocumented Migrants Are Charged with Capital Murder," *CNN*, June 26, 2024, https://www.cnn.com/2024/06/26/us/jocelyn-nun garay-killing-houston/index.html.

63. Rosalind Adams and Gwynne Hogan, "Sexual Harassment at NYC Shelter for Migrant Families Went Unchecked for Months," *The City — NYC*, June 27, 2023, https://www.thecity.nyc/2023/06/27/sexual-harass ment-brooklyn-migrant-shelter/.

64. Elizabeth Heckman, "Young Migrants Tied to 'Shocking'

Increase in Gang-Led Crime in NYC's Times Square, Says NYPD," *Fox News*, October 16, 2024, https://www.foxnews.com/media/young-migrants-tied-shocking-increase-gang-led-crime-nycs-times-square-nypd; Craig McCarthy and Matt Troutman, "Shocking Data Detail NYC Illegal Migrant Crime with 3.2K Arrests — Including Assault, Robbery, Murder," *New York Post*, May 2, 2025, https://nypost.com/2025/05/02/us-news/shocking-data-details-nyc-illegal-migrant-crime-with-3-2k-arrests-including-assault-robbery-murder/.

65. Hannah Davis, "Increased Illegal Immigration Brings Increased Crime: Almost Two-Thirds of Federal Arrests Involve Noncitizens," *The Heritage Foundation*, June 20, 2023, https://www.heritage.org/crime-and-justice/ commentary/increased-illegal-immigration-brings-increased-crime-almost-23-federal. See also: Steven Malanga, "No, You're Not Imagining a Migrant Crime Spree," *City Journal*, Autumn 2024, https://www.city-journal.org/ article/no-youre-not-imagining-a-migrant-crime-spree.

66. "Florida Crash: Indian Trucker, Harjinder Singh, Who Killed 3, Fails English, Road Tests; Answered Only 2 Questions Correctly," *Times of India*, updated August 20, 2025, https://timesofindia.indiatimes.com/world/us/harjinder-singh-indian-truck-driver-uturn-accident-minivan-in-florida-3-killed-donald-trump-administration-criticised-california-governor-gavin-n-ewsom/articleshow/123377891.cms.

67. "Canadian Truck Driver of Indian Origin Pleads Guilty in Crash That Killed Olympian," *Moneycontrol*, February 12, 2026, https://www.moneycontrol.com/world/canadian-truck-driver-of-indian-origin-pleads-guilty-in-crash-that-killed-olympian-article-13824204.html.

68. Peter Pinedo, "Blue State in Hot Seat After ICE Busts Illegal Immigrant with No Name Given License," *Fox News*, October 7, 2025, https://www. foxnews.com/politics/blue-state-hot-seat-after-ice-busts-illegal-immigrant-with-no-name-given-license.

69. Statistics Canada, *Census Profile, 2021 Census of Population: Immigration and Citizenship by Place of Birth and Generation Status: Peel Region, Mississauga, and Brampton, Ontario* (Ottawa: Statistics Canada, 2022), https://www12. statcan.gc.ca/census-recensement/2021/dp-pd/prof/index.cfm?Lang=E.

70. For example: Gaurav Kumar, "18 Including Indian-Origin Men Held as Peel Police Bust Organised Crime Targeting South Asian Businesses in Canada," *India Today*, June 17, 2025, https://www.indiatoday.in/world/canada-news/story/indi-origin-among-18-held-peel-region-police-bust-organised-crime-against-south-asians-businesses-canada-brampton-2742184-2025-06-17; Adrian Humphreys, "Ontario Man Named Boss of Huge Cross-Border Drug Smuggling Ring Slipped Out of Canada and into U.S. Court," *National Post*, February 10, 2025,

https://nationalpost.com/news/ontario-trucker-cocaine-2.

71. Toronto Police Service, "Auto Theft Home Invasion Prevention Tips," *Toronto Police Service Newsroom*, March 13, 2024, https://www.tps.ca/media-centre/stories/auto-theft-home-invasion-prevention-tips/.

72. Statistics Canada, "Focus on Geography Series, 2021 Census of Population: Surrey (City), British Columbia," *Statistics Canada*, https://www12.statcan.gc.ca/census-recensement/2021/as-sa/fogs-spg/page.cfm?Lang=E&dguid=2021A00055915004&topic=9.

73. Jupinderjit Singh, "Canada: Punjabi Gangsters Behind Surge in Extortion Threats, Surrey Declares Emergency," *The Tribune India*, January 27, 2026, https://www.tribuneindia.com/news/punjab/punjabi-gangsters-behind-surge-in-extortion-threats-canadas-surrey-declares-emergency.

74. "13 Members of 'Violent Criminal Network' Arrested by Peel Police After Home Invasions," *CP24 News*, March 20, 2025, YouTube video, 2:15, https://www.youtube.com/watch?v=ubB-Y008WRc.

75. Statistics Denmark, *Immigrants and Descendants of Immigrants: Crime and Justice 2021* (Copenhagen: Statistics Denmark, 2022), https://www.dst.dk/ en/Statistik/emner/sociale-forhold/kriminalitet.

76. Statistics Finland, *Statistics on Offences and Coercive Measures 2023* (Helsinki: Tilastokeskus, 2024), https://stat.fi/til/rpk/2023/01/rpk_2023_01_2024-04-18_tie_001_en.html.

77. Swedish National Council for Crime Prevention (Brå), *Overrepresentation in Registered Crime* (Stockholm: Brottsförebyggande rådet, 2022), https:// bra.se/publikationer/arkiv/publikationer/2022-12-14-overrepresentation-i-registrerad-brottslighet.html.

78. Statistics Norway, *Immigrants and Crime 2022* (Oslo: Statistisk sentralbyrå, 2023), https://www.ssb.no/sosiale-forhold-og-kriminalitet/kriminalitet-og-rettsvesen/statistikk/innvandrere-og-kriminalitet.

79. Federal Crime Office (BKA), *Federal Situation Report Crime 2023* (Wiesbaden: Bundeskriminalamt, 2024), https://www.bka.de/EN/ CurrentInformation/Statistics/PoliceCrime Statistics/2023/pcs2023.html.

80. French Ministry of the Interior, *Insecurity and Delinquency Figures 2022* (Paris: Ministère de l'Intérieur, 2023), https://www.interieur.gouv.fr / actualites/actualites-du-ministere/chiffres-cles-de-la-delinquance-et-de-la-criminalite-enregistrees-en-france-en.

81. UK Home Office, *Crime in England and Wales: Year Ending March 2023* (London: Home Office, 2023), https://www.gov.uk/government/statistics/ crime-in-england-and-wales-year-ending-march-2023.

82. Office for National Statistics, *Religion, England and Wales: Census 2021* (2022), https://www.ons.gov.uk/peoplepopul ationandcommunity/ culturalidentity/religion/bulletins/re ligionenglandandwales/census2021.

83. Home Office, *Operation of Police Powers Under the Terrorism Act 2000: Quarterly Update to March 2025*, Table P.0 1 (2025), https://www.gov.uk/government/ statistics/oper ation-of-police-powers-under-tact-2000-to-march-2025.

84. Ran Abramitzky, Leah Boustan, and Katherine Eriksson, "To the New World and Back Again: Return Migrants in the Age of Mass Migration," *Industrial and Labor Relations Review* 72, no. 2 (2019): 300–322, https://doi. org/10.117 7/0019793917726981.

85. Tristin Hopper, "Canadians Now Spending $1 Billion per Year to Cover Health-Care Costs of Refugee Claimants," National Post, February 17, 2026, https://nationalpost.com/opinion/canadians-now-spending -1-billion-per-year-to-cover-health-care-costs-of-refugee-clai mants.

86. For example: Government of Canada, *Resettlement Assistance Program (RAP)*, Immigration, Refugees and Citizenship Canada, last modified September 26, 2024, https://www.canada.ca/en/immigration-refugees-citizenshi p/services/refugees/help-within-canada/government-assiste d-refugee-program.html; Government of Canada, *Immigration Loans Program (ILP)*, Immigration, Refugees and Citizenship Canada,

https://www.canada.ca/en/immigration-refugees-citizenship/corporate/transparency/access-information-privacy/info-source/institutional-functions-programs-activities.html; Government of Canada, *The Refugee Settlement Journey: From Arrival to Citizenship*, Immigration, Refugees and Citizenship Canada, 2017, https://www.canada.ca/content/dam/ircc/migration/ircc/english/pdf/pub/settlement-journey-eng.pdf.

87. Employment and Social Development Canada, "Helping Families Get Ahead with a More Generous Canada Child Benefit," news release, Peterborough, Ontario, July 18, 2025, https://www.canada.ca/en/employment-social-development/news/2025/07/helping-families-get-ahead-with-a-more-generous-canada-child-benefit.html.

88. For example, City of Ottawa, "Child Care Fee Subsidy," *Ottawa.ca*, https:// ottawa.ca/en/family-and-social-services/childrens-services/child-care-fee-subsidy.

89. Jamie Sarkonak, @sarkonakj, "(Post of a Hindi Video Explaining How Indian Citizens Living in Canada Can Claim the Canada Child Benefit)," *X (formerly Twitter)*, February 9, 2026, https://x.com/sarkonakj/ status/2020941673568903391.

90. James P. Smith and Barry Edmonston, eds., *The New Americans: Economic, Demographic, and Fiscal Effects of Immigration* (Washington, DC: National Academy Press, 1997), https://doi.org/10.17226/5779.

91. Ibid. See also: Peter Brimelow, "George Borjas On the Media's Immigration Economics: 'People Now Are Getting That It's Complete Nonsense,'" *VDARE*, December 26, 2007, https://vdare.com/articles/george-borjas-on-the-media-s-im migration-economics-people-now-are-getting-that-it-s-com plete-nonsense.

92. Smith and Edmonston, *The New Americans*, 277–280; Brimelow, "George Borjas On the Media's Immigration Economics."

93. Brimelow, "George Borjas On the Media's Immigration Economics."

94. George J. Borjas, "Immigration and the American Worker: A Review of the Academic Literature," *Center for Immigration Studies*, April 9, 2013, https://cis.org/Report/Immigration -and-American-Worker; George J. Borjas, *Immigration Economics* (Cambridge, MA: Harvard University Press, 2014).

95. Ibid.

96. Ibid. See also: George Borjas, "The Labor Demand Curve Is Downward Sloping: Reexamining the Impact of Immigration on the Labor Market," *Quarterly Journal of Economics* 118, no. 4 (2003): 1335–1374. https:// scholar.harvard.edu /sites/scholar.harvard.edu/files/gborjas/files/qje2003.pdf.

97. Abdurrahman Aydemir and George J. Borjas, "Cross-Coun try Variation in the Impact of International Migration:

Canada, Mexico, and the United States," *Journal of the European Economic Association* 5, no. 4 (June 2007): 663–708, https://scholar.harvard.edu/files/gborjas/files/jeea2007.pdf.

98. Patrick Grady and Herbert Grubel, *Immigration and the Welfare State Revisited: Fiscal Transfers to Immigrants in Canada in 2014* (Vancouver: Fraser Institute, November 2015), https://www.fraserinstitute.org/sites/default/files/immigration-and-the-welfare-state-revisited.pdf.

99. Danish Ministry of Finance, *Immigrants' Net Contribution to the Public Finances in Denmark* (Copenhagen: Ministry of Finance, 2021), fremskrivning-af-indvandreres-nettobidrag-til-de-offentlige-finanser_oea_maj-2018.pdf.

100. Daiva Kancs and Patrizio Lecca, *Long-Term Social, Economic and Fiscal Effects of Immigration into the EU Member States* (Brussels: European Commission, Joint Research Centre, 2017), https://publications.jrc.ec.europa.eu/ repository/handle/JRC107441.

101. Migration Observatory, *Asylum and Refugee Resettlement in the UK*, Briefing (Oxford: University of Oxford, 2022), https://migrationobservatory.ox.ac. uk/resources/briefings/migration-to-the-uk-asylum/.

102. House of Commons Library, *Asylum Statistics*, Briefing Paper CBP-9078, 3rd ed. (London: UK Parliament, 2025), https://commonslibrary.parliament.uk/ research-briefings/sn01403/.

103. Douglas Porter and Robert Kavcic, "Catch-'23: Canada's Affordability Conundrum," *BMO Economics*, May 26, 2023, https://economics.bmo.com/ en/publications/detail/34d60afc-5f9d-4110-a19b-ba9b160782f2/.

104. Douglas Todd, "How Migration Impacts Vancouver's Housing Prices," *Vancouver Sun*, October 11, 2024, https://vancouversun.com/opinion / columnists/douglas-todd-how-migration-impacts-vancouvers-housing-prices.

105. Diane Francis, "Canada's Health System Can't Support Immigrant Influx: Simply Piling More People into an Already-Flailing System Is Irresponsible," *Financial Post*, November 30, 2022, https://financialpost.com/diane-francis/canada-health-system-cant-support-immigrant-influx.

106. Ibrahim Mahmoud and Xiang-yu Hou, "Immigrants and the Utilization of Hospital Emergency Departments," *World Journal of Emergency Medicine* 3, no. 4 (2012), https://pmc.ncbi.nlm.nih.gov/articles/PMC4129805/.

107. I'm grateful to Pastor Doug Wilson, Christ Church, Moscow, Idaho for this phrasing which I believe he coined.

108. International Monetary Fund, *World Economic Outlook Database*, April 2025 (Washington, DC: IMF, 2025), https://www.imf.org/en/Publications/WEO.

109. World Economic Forum, *The Future of Jobs Report 2020* (Geneva: World Economic Forum, 2020), 11–13, http

s://www.weforum.org/publications/ the-future-of-jobs-report-2020/.

110. Elon Musk, interview by Tesla Investor Relations, Q3 2025 Earnings Call, October 23, 2025, as cited in *Humanoids Daily*, "Tesla Targets 1 Million Unit Optimus Production Line, V3 Prototype Set for Q1," November 7, 2025, https://www.humanoidsdaily.com/feed/tesla-targets -1-million-unit-optimus-line-v3-prototype-q1.

111. U.S. Department of State, *2023 Report on International Religious Freedom: Saudi Arabia* (2023), https://www.state.gov/reports/2023-report-on-int ernational-religious-freedom/saudi-arabia.

112. In the province of Quebec in Canada, French is the dominant language and proficiency in that language could serve as the criterion.

113. Viola Rita, "Spotting Lies with Artificial Intelligence," *Nature*, 14 February 2024, https://www.nature.com/articles/d 43978-024-00029-y.

Postscript—A Final Word and a Beginning

If you've reached this postscript, you've done more than finish a book. You've wrestled with an argument about how North American society can be restored—how it might recover unity, trust, justice, and prosperity. If you've been convinced that a resurgence of Traditional Conservatism is what's needed, a final step awaits. This postscript exists for one reason: to turn conviction into connection, and connection into action.

What you have encountered in these pages was never meant to be practiced in isolation, but to be embodied together. Beyond these words are others who have read what you have read and felt what you have felt—perhaps recognizing, "This names what I have been reaching for." This postscript is an invitation to find one another, to meet, to organize, to encourage one another, and to act together—locally and beyond. It also opens an ongoing channel between us, so that this book is not the end of the conversation but the beginning of a shared one. As a first step, our movement needs a name—something it's called and something we can call each other. The immediate thought might be to call the movement Traditional Conservatism and its followers traditional conservatives. While those labels are accurate, they leave the movement vulnerable to mischaracterization because both *traditional* and *conservative*—even when linked together—are already widely used in public discourse to describe positions, instincts, and coalitions that diverge in important ways from the specific philosophical commitments defined in this book.

We need a label that clearly signals that the form of traditional conservatism advanced by this movement is defined and disciplined by the framework set out in this book. The front cover states the crisis facing both America and Canada—*Christ or Collapse*. Inside, Part One is titled *Our Christian Foundation: Principles, History, & Rationale* and introduces the proposed solution. The back cover expresses the remedy most plainly: *Restoring the Foundation for a Flourishing Nation*. Together, these titles leave no ambiguity about the movement's purpose: restoring the Christian foundations on which unity, peace, and prosperity depend. For that reason, I propose we call our cause the **Foundationalist movement**, or simply **Foundationalism**, and its adherents **Foundationalists**. All Foundationalists are traditional conservatives, but not all traditional conservatives are Foundationalists.

A bit more clarification is needed. There's a branch of philosophy called epistemology, which studies how we come to know things. Within that field is a view known as foundationalism. It maintains that certain beliefs must be self-evident or verifiable, and that all other beliefs derive their justification from these basic truths—much as a house rests upon its foundation. I point this out because our Foundationalism is not that foundationalism. While there are similarities, the political Foundationalism advanced in this book is not intended as a direct extension, reinterpretation, or application of epistemological foundationalism. In some cases, the prefix "political" could be added for precision, but given the relatively low public profile of epistemological foundationalism—and the absence of any social movement associated with it—such a prefix is generally unnecessary when the term is used in context. Having established that we are (political) Foundationalists, I invite you, warmly and wholeheartedly, to take the next step to join us at <u>FoundationalistHub.org</u>

At FoundationalistHub.org you can join our mailing list to receive new writings, reflections, and announcements, including updates on conferences and conventions. You'll be added to a directory and matched with members in local and regional groups already meeting. Once you've found your people, you'll encourage one another, share experiences, and organize collaborative initiatives to advance the Foundationalist vision of traditional conservatism. It's important to note that not every group in this network will be newly formed; some communities may already exist and simply find renewed purpose or clarity through the Foundationalist vision. These groups don't need to reorganize or adopt a new name. It's enough that they mindfully put the Foundationalist principles into practice within their existing structures, deepening their impact and aligning their efforts with the broader enterprise.

And now, to work.